Battlegr

BULLECOURT

Other guides in the Battleground Europe Series:

Walking the Salient *by* Paul Reed
Ypres - Sanctuary Wood and Hooge *by* Nigel Cave
Ypres - Hill 60 *by* Nigel Cave
Ypres - Messines Ridge *by* Peter Oldham

Walking the Somme *by* Paul Reed
Somme - Gommecourt *by* Nigel Cave
Somme - Serre *by* Jack Horsfall & Nigel Cave
Somme - Beaumont Hamel *by* Nigel Cave
Somme - Thiepval *by* Michael Stedman
Somme - La Boisselle *by* Michael Stedman
Somme - Fricourt *by* Michael Stedman
Somme - Carnoy-Montauban *by* Graham Maddocks
Somme - Pozières *by* Graham Keech
Somme - Courcelette *by* Paul Reed
Somme - Boom Ravine *by* Trevor Pidgeon
Somme - Mametz Wood *by* Michael Renshaw
Somme - Advance to Victory (North) 1918 *by* Michael Stedman

Arras - Vimy Ridge *by* Nigel Cave

Hindenburg Line *by* Peter Oldham
Epehy *by* Bill Mitchenson
Riqueval *by* Bill Mitchenson

Boer War - The Relief of Ladysmith, Colenso, Spion Kop *by* Lewis Childs

Accrington Pals Trail *by* WilliamTurner

Poets at War: Wilfred Owen *by* Helen McPhail and Philip Guest

Gallipoli *by* Nigel Steel

Battleground Europe Series guides in preparation:

Ypres - Polygon Wood *by* Nigel Cave
La Bassée - Givenchy *by* Michael Orr
La Bassée - Neuve Chapelle 1915 *by* Geoff Bridger
Walking Arras *by* Paul Reed
Arras - Monchy le Preux *by* Colin Fox
Somme - Following the Ancre *by* Michael Stedman
Somme - High Wood *by* Terry Carter
Somme - Advance to Victory 1918 *by* Michael Stedman
Somme - Ginchy *by* Michael Stedman
Somme - Combles *by* Paul Reed
Somme - Beaucourt *by* Michael Renshaw

Walking Verdun *by* Paul Reed

Poets at War: Edmund Blunden *by* Helen McPhail and Philip Guest

Boer War - The Siege of Ladysmith *by* Lewis Childs
Isandhlwana *by* Ian Knight and Ian Castle
Rorkes Drift *by* Ian Knight and Ian Castle

With the continued expansion of the Battleground series a Battleground Europe Club has been formed to benefit the reader. The purpose of the Club is to keep members informed of new titles and key developments by way of a quarterly newsletter, and to offer many other reader-benefits. Membership is free and by registering an interest you can help us predict print runs and thus maintain prices at their present levels. Please call the office 01226 734555, or send your name and address along with a request for more information to:

Battleground Europe Club
Pen & Sword Books Ltd, 47 Church Street, Barnsley, South Yorkshire S70 2AS

Battleground Europe

BULLECOURT

GRAHAM KEECH

Series editor
Nigel Cave

LEO COOPER

First published in 1999 by
LEO COOPER
an imprint of
Pen Sword Books Limited
47 Church Street, Barnsley, South Yorkshire S70 2AS

ISBN 0 85052 652 3

A CIP catalogue of this book is available
from the British Library

Printed by Redwood Books Limited
Trowbridge, Wiltshire

*For up-to-date information on other titles produced under the Leo Cooper imprint,
please telephone or write to:*
Pen & Sword Books Ltd, FREEPOST, 47 Church Street
Barnsley, South Yorkshire S70 2AS
Telephone 01226 734222

CONTENTS

Rue d'Arras, Bullecourt, before the war.

INTRODUCTION BY SERIES EDITOR

Of all the villages along what was known to the British as the Hindenburg Line, Bullecourt is perhaps the best known, albeit usually only as a name. It does not receive that many visitors, though it has been a place of pilgrimage for Australians for many years, culminating in the erection of the Digger statue in 1992. Bullecourt has also been fortunate is the great interest shown in its wartime past by the people of the village and the Arras branch of *Souvenir Francais*. It was here that the first of the Western Front Association plaques was placed, associating itself with the cross memorial erected by *Souvenir Francais.*

This small agricultural village, one of many in this region which devoted itself largely to sugar production, was the centre of Fifth Army's efforts during the Battle of Arras in April and May 1917. The fight here is inextricably linked with that very controversial soldier, General Sir Hubert Gough, and with members of the Australian Imperial Force. The bitterness that this battle engendered amongst Australians towards British senior command is only equalled by the action at Fromelles – even Pozières, on the Somme, does not seem to rate so highly. Gallipoli, of course, is a story of its own.

Ruined houses in Bullecourt. The pond was close to the modern church. German official photograph. IWMQ45616

Although this is a notable battle in the history of Australian arms, it also witnessed a most significant British presence, not least in the controversial use of tanks. All too often the fact that Bullecourt was part of the much larger Battle of Arras is forgotten; indeed this latter battle is still all too little known, despite the accessible and useful account *(Cheerful Sacrifice)* written in recent years by Jonathan Nicholls.

The fact remains that Bullecourt has a certain integrity all of its own – and its close association with the Australian Imperial Force assists this. The ground seems to have changed little, and certain key features – such as the railway embankment, many of the roads and the tracks – provide the topographical continuity which assists in trying to understand actions taken and orders given so many years ago. Graham Keech has used his capacity for knowledge, and grasp, of detail to apply it to the ground. The large number of situation maps and the excellent and full touring section should help to make sense of what can be a very difficult series of engagements to follow – with multiple British attacks, Australian attacks and German counter-attacks.

It is a battlefield that is now quiet and allows for reflection; evocative and daunting. Its cemeteries are not nearly as frequently visited as those on the Somme or the Salient. The series has now begun to turn its attention to this and other neglected areas that saw the armies of Britain and its Dominions fight so vigorously. The Hindenburg Line is now well covered; it is the turn of those small villages and hamlets lying in the semicircle around the historic centre of Arras to have their tragic histories explored and to bring, one can hope, more people to come to them to reflect on the sacrifice of a generation that is all but disappeared. It should be one of the aims of a book such as this to ensure that new generations can study the battlefield and think, rather than walk away with an impression of futility caused, say, by a visit to the cemeteries, an oversimplified popular history and the hindsight which tells that the Great War led to the horrors of the Second World War.

Nigel Cave
Ely Place, London

AUTHOR'S INTRODUCTION

The name Bullecourt remains, in the minds of ordinary Australians, the third element in a trilogy of British command blunders. After the experiences of Fromelles and Pozières in 1916 the first battle of Bullecourt, in April 1917, is remembered as a battle that need not have been fought. It was conceived to aid the British Third Army fighting around Arras. If it had to be fought, it should have been better planned and preparations should have been more thorough. The Commander of the British Fifth Army, General Sir Hubert Gough, insisted on attacking at a re-entrant against all military logic. Further, he placed too much confidence in the words of a relatively junior tank officer who insisted that the new weapon was capable of reducing the belts of wire in front of the Hindenburg Line. On 10 April, when the tanks failed to arrive at the allotted time, the proposed attack was cancelled but rescheduled twenty-four hours later. This short delay, considered by the Australian commanders to be inadequate, was insisted upon by Gough with the knowledge and support of the Commander-in Chief Field Marshall Sir Douglas Haig. As a consequence the troops, who went forward the next morning, were tired and sorely in need of rest. As in all the battles fought during the years 1914 to 1918 lack of communication between the men right at the front and those further back caused immense difficulties. When the tanks either failed or were subject to erroneous reports the Australians, held up near the two lines of Hindenburg trenches, were denied artillery support for fear of hitting friendly troops.

The second battle of Bullecourt which opened on 3 May 1917 was generally better planned. It was part of a wider operation but was still launched in an unfavourable

8

position for the attacking troops, and was to be prolonged, this in an effort to help the French. In recent years a reassessment of the roles played by the senior Australian officers, particularly in the planning and early stages of the second battle, has removed some of the criticism previously levelled at the British commanders.

In the two battles of Bullecourt the four Australian divisions involved: the 4th, the 2nd, the 1st and the 5th, lost a total of 10,000 casualties. Of these about 3,000 occurred in the first battle and about 7,000 in the second.

Whilst in no way disputing the contribution made by the Australians it should not be forgotten that three British divisions were also involved at Bullecourt. On 10 April the 62nd (West Riding) Division lost heavily due to mistakes in the interpretation of orders. In the second battle the 62nd Division was again involved as were the 7th Division and the 58th (London) Division.

The fight in Bullecourt

Signposted trail through the Australian battlefield

An historic trail

A walking tour
Starting Point : Bullecourt
a 8 km lap - 2 hours
a 13 km lap - 3 hours and 15 min.

Today the inhabitants still remember the sacrifices that were made and the fearsome fighting which occurred all around. On the Saturday nearest to Anzac Day, 25 April, each year a programme of remembrance is held in Bullecourt. An excellent museum put together by M. Letaille, originally housed in the Mairie, can now be visited at M. Letaille's the home, No. 1 Rue d'Arras, Bullecourt. There is also a sign-posted trail through the Australian battlefield, with an accompanying English language leaflet, copies of which can be obtained from the museum in Bullecourt or by post from Les Amis de la Nature, 127 Rue du Cdt Dumetz, 62000 Arras.

Over many years M. and Mme Letaille and M. and Mme Durand have welcomed visitors to the battlefield and given freely of their time to help and inform. In recognition, both couples, have been presented with the insignia of the Order of Australia.

ACKNOWLEDGEMENTS

When collecting material for a book which deals with events in a particular location, there is no greater help than to be able to meet and talk with people who live in the area concerned. I am therefore extremely grateful to Derek Holgate who accompanied me to France to introduce me to M. and Mme. Durand in Hendecourt and M. and Mme. Letaille in Bullecourt. Both M. and Mme. Durand and M. and Mme. Letaille were most generous in offering me hospitality, information and the loan of materials, some of which have been incorporated in the text.

In the course of the research I have made a number of visits to the Public Record Office at Kew. I would like to express my appreciation to all the staff there who have assisted me with accessing maps and files. In particular I would like to thank Nick Forbes for his help over the difficult question of Copyright. Crown copyright material in the Public Record Office is reproduced by permission of the Controller of Her Majesty's Stationery Office.

I wish to express my thanks to the Trustees of the Imperial War

Museum for permission to reproduce a number of photographs from the museum's photographic archive. In this context I should also like to thank Ian Carter for his advice and help in the actual choice of photographs. I would also like to thank all the staff of the museum reading room who helped me by finding numerous books and maps.

I am very grateful to David Fletcher, curator, of the Tank Museum at Bovington for allowing me access to Tank Corps files and for explaining some of the finer points of early tank construction and the idiosyncrasies of their running. I am also indebted to the museum for allowing me reproduce certain tank photographs.

I would also like to record my thanks to: Colin Fox for translating German records, Mrs

Chapel in Bullecourt on the rue d' Arras.

K Kidby of the British Library for help on Newspaper Copyright, Colonel Terry Cave for the loan of maps and documents, James Brazier for 'editorial advice', Philip Guest for bringing the 'dead mule' story to my attention, and to all the staff at Commonwealth War Graves Commission who provided information on soldiers and cemeteries.

Finally, but by no means least, I would like to thank Nigel Cave for his help and advice as Series Editor and to Paul and Roni Wilkinson and all the staff at Pen & Sword in Barnsley.

ADVICE TO TRAVELLERS

Even after 80 years the battlefields of the World War 1 can still be dangerous. So don't, on any account, move or even touch items such as shell and grenades placed by the side of fields for collection by the French authorities. Even if such items of ordnance are ignored it is still

11

Temporary buildings, for the schools and Mairie, during the reconstruction of the village in the 1920s.

advisable, as with any foreign travel, to go well insured. For reciprocal medical cover be sure to take Form E 111, which can be obtained from Post Offices. Full personal insurance and breakdown cover for your vehicle can be obtained through the AA or RAC. In addition, obtain a Green Card, from your insurance company, to extend your vehicle insurance for the countries to be visited. Many companies no longer actually issue a card but require to be informed of the dates of the trip and the countries involved.

Always go prepared for extremes of weather, even in the middle of summer, with warm and waterproof clothing. Walking boots are advisable as farm tracks can be both muddy and rutted and, accidents easily happen. There are no cafés in the middle of battlefields. The most convenient alternative, and the one that means that you can devote as much time as possible to walking the ground, is to take a picnic lunch. Food and drink can be bough in shops in Bapaume. There is a bar in Bullecourt 'Le Canberra', 36 Route de Douai, almost opposite the church. It is run by Mme. Sylvie Delatte, who does not sell food but will permit you to eat your picnic in the bar provided you purchase some drinks.

To reach Bullecourt takes about two hours from Calais using the Paris Motorway. Leave the A1 at junction 14 (Bapaume) and at the roundabout turn right and take the N30 to Fremicourt/Hermies. At Beugny turn left on to the D20 to Vaulx-Vraucourt. At Vaulx-Vraucourt take the CD956 to Ecoust-St-Mein (beware of the dangerous road junction) and then the D 36 to Mory and Ervillers. Turn right on to the D956 to Ecoust-St-Mein. At Ecoust-St-Mein bear right on to the N 356 to Bullecourt and Douai.

In addition to the IGN Blue Series map 2507 O (Croisilles) the

Green Series map No 4 Laon-Arras will be useful. If you are intending to visit cemeteries not mentioned in the text the Michelin Map No 53, overprinted with war cemeteries and memorials, is a must. This can be obtained from the Commonwealth War Graves Commission, Maidenhead, Berks.

Accommodation is available in Bapaume, Albert and some of the nearby villages. A full list of all types of accommodation can be obtained from:

Comité Regional du Tourisme de Picardie, 3 Rue Vincent Auriol, 80000 Amiens Tel: 00 33 322 91 10 15.

The following short list may be useful.

Hotels:
Hotel de la Paix, 43 Rue Victor Hugo, 80300 Albert.
Tel: 322 75 01 64.
Hotel de la Basilique, 3-5 Rue Gambetta, 80300 Albert.
Tel: 322 75 37 00.
Hotel la Paix, 11 Avenue Abel Guidet, 62450 Bapaume.
Tel: 321 07 11 03.

Bed & Breakfast:
Sommecourt, 39 Grand Rue, 80300 Courcelette.
Tel: 322 74 01 35 Paul Reed and Kieron Murphy.
Les Galets, Route de Beaumont, Auchonvillers 80560.
Tel: 322 76 28 79 Mike & Julie Renshaw.
10 Rue Delattre Auchonvillers 80560.
Tel: 322 76 23 66 Avril Williams.

Rue de Quéant during the reconstruction of the village.

LIST OF MAPS

14

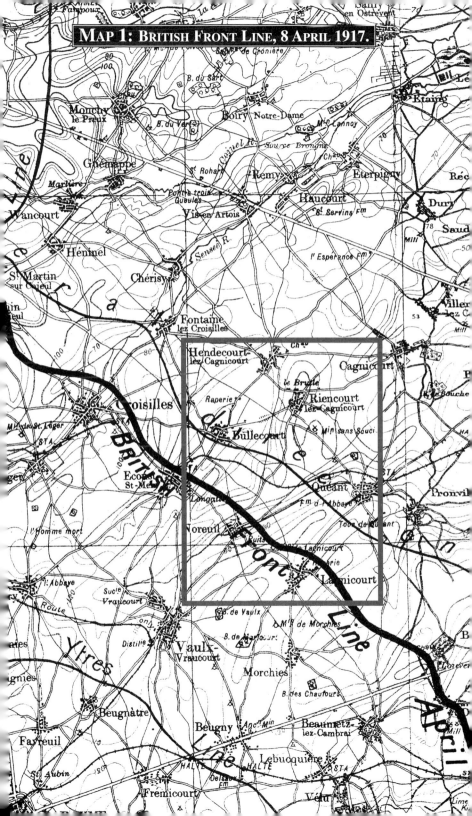

MAP 1: BRITISH FRONT LINE, 8 APRIL 1917.

Chapter One

MILITARY AND POLITICAL CHANGES: AUTUMN AND WINTER 1916/17

The Battle of the Somme drew to a close in November 1916. In the period from 1 July to 16 November the approximate casualties were, on the German side 670,000, and on the British and French side 630,000, giving the Allies a significant advantage in the numbers killed, wounded, captured or missing. At the beginning of the year the German Army was still very strong but, by November, the need to expand and to use experienced officers to form new staffs and formations, together with the losses on the Somme, had reduced it to a state which lead inexorably to its defeat in 1918. When the fighting died down, the British set about a programme to consolidate the new front line and to turn captured German fortifications into accommodation for allied soldiers.

On 15 and 16 November a conference of allied military leaders was held at Chantilly, chaired by General Joffre. Agreement was reached on maintaining offensive operations during the winter of 1916/17, as and when the weather permitted, and preparations were to be made to resume full operations from the beginning of the following February. The British were to be responsible for the major part of the offensive. Joffre was concerned that, after Verdun, the French army was in no state to undertake a large attack. The plan envisaged attacking the enemy in two salients: the one created at the end of the Somme battles and the larger one further south near the Aisne **(See map 2)**. The British would attack in the north using the four armies, the First, Third, Fourth and Fifth and, at the same time, the French Groupe des Armées du Nord (G.A.N.) was to advance with two armies, the Tenth and the Sixth, between the Somme and Lassigny, both operations to commence on 1 February. Fourteen days later, the French Fifth Army part of the Groupe des Armées du Centre (G.A.C.) would attack on the Aisne. In the summer, the British would launch their planned offensive in Belgium to reduce the threat of submarine attacks from bases in northern Belgium.

On the same days, i.e. 15 and 16 November 1916, an inter-allied conference of political leaders was held in Paris. Among those present was David Lloyd George, British Secretary of State for War, a position he had held since July 1916. He was strongly of the opinion that the

GENERAL JOFFRE'S PROJECTED OFFENSIVE FOR 1917

MAP 2

General Joffre

Somme offensive had been kept going too long. Although wishing to prosecute the war with vigour he had no faith in the existing military policies and strategies. When the Paris conference failed to take control over the military, Lloyd George set in train a series of events which led, in early December, to the resignation of Herbert Asquith, and the creation of a War Cabinet, with himself as Prime Minister.

Meanwhile, in France, change was also taking place. General Joffre was limogé, i.e. compelled to resign, and raised to the rank of Marshal of France, a title which had not been used since the disastrous war of 1870. A new War Cabinet was created with Aristide Briand as Premier and Minister of Foreign Affairs and General Lyautey as Minister of War. Joffre was replaced by Robert Nivelle, the relatively young, 60-year-old, hero

17

David Lloyd George

of Fort Douaumont. He was a man of winning personality who, as a result of having an English mother, had the distinct advantage of being able to speak perfect English.

Nivelle convinced Briand that Joffre's plan for combined Franco-British attacks in the spring, to be followed by the summer attack in Belgium, should be replaced. In its stead he proposed that the British should extend their line south of the Somme to Roye, and confine their attacks to a smaller area around Arras. The French would launch the major attack between Reims and Soissons on the Aisne, using the newly created Groupe des Armées de Réserve, (G.A.R.) a few days after the British attack and a subsidiary attack by G.A.N., between the Oise and the Avre **(See map 3)**. Whereas Joffre's plan envisaged a wearing down of the enemy's powers of resistance, Nivelle expected to destroy the enemy forces in a major battle. The break through should be achieved in twenty-four to forty-eight hours and if not the offensive would be stopped.

Such was Nivelle's confidence and magnetism that he won over the suspicious British Prime Minister to his cause. Lloyd George was so taken with the plan that he agreed, without consulting either the British Commander-in-Chief, Field-Marshal Sir Douglas Haig, or the Chief of the Imperial General Staff, General Sir William Robertson, to the subordination of the British Army, i.e. Haig, to Nivelle. This was sprung upon the two British military leaders at the Calais conference on 26 February 1917, a conference which had been called to discuss problems of transport in northern France! Subsequently, this decision was modified, placing Haig under the general direction of Nivelle for the period of the forthcoming offensive, but with the right of appeal to the British government if he felt that the orders received jeopardised the safety of his army.

As plans for the offensive went forward the Germans were also reviewing their options. That they had suffered mightily on the Somme was in no doubt and conditions at home were deteriorating. The winter line held on the Somme was a poor one, forced on them by the continuation of the fighting into November. There was no defence in depth. Ludendorff, in contrast with Falkenhayn, did not have any objection to vacating ground, if by so doing he could materially improve his position. Falkenhayn's doctrine, propounded in 1915, as a result of the stalemate created by the failure of the German offensive in 1914, required the creation of a strong foremost line. This line, which should be capable of withstanding attack by superior numbers, was to be held at all costs, and if any section was captured it was to be

GENERAL NIVELLE'S PROJECTED OFFENSIVE FOR 1917

SCALE OF MILES

MAP 3

General Robert Nivelle, Commander-in-Chief of the the French Army 1917

retaken at once. By September 1916 Ludendorff and Hindenburg were aware of the problems of manpower and supplies that would intensify in the following year. The allied blockade was crippling German industrial production whilst at the same time the seas were fully open to allied shipping. The United States was also giving help on a large scale. With these difficulties in mind construction was begun of powerful rear positions in the west: the Siegfried-Stellung, running from Arras, west of Cambrai, St. Quentin La Fère to Vailly-sur-Aisne. It was this system, that became known to the Allies as the Hindenburg Line. The word 'line' was inappropriate, since the Siegfried-Stellung was in fact not a line but a defensive zone on the whole of the British front, except on the northern sector between Quéant and Neuville Vitasse **(See maps 4&7)**. At Quéant it was joined by the Wotan-Stellung, which ran southwards from Drocourt, and was known to the

19

British as the Drocourt-Quéant Switch. From Quéant southwards there existed a second system about a mile and a half behind the front line and consisted of fire and support trenches separated by a gap of about two hundred yards. This was the original Hindenburg Line which, when inspected by Colonel Fritz von Lossberg, Chief of Staff of the German First Army, was found to be sited on the forward slope rather than the reverse slope. He insisted that the line be repositioned approximately three thousand yards further forward, and that an outpost system be included in front of the new line.

At the same time, artillery, machine guns and infantry were positioned to create a broad belt of defences. Once the enemy was past the outpost line, he would be out of sight of, and the protection of, his own artillery but in full view of that of the defenders, along with their mortars and machine guns. The new position was in accordance with the system of defence in depth introduced by General Ludendorff. The old line became the support position and the artillery protection line. Each system was protected by tracts of wire generally in three belts, each ten to fifteen yards in depth and about five yards apart. In front of the fire trench they were arranged in a zigzag pattern to permit patrols to enter and leave the lines but also to channel attackers into the zones of fire of carefully-sited machine guns. The existence of the new line was finally established by the British in late February 1917, although the first indications had been obtained by aerial photography as far back as the end of October 1916. It was unfortunate that weather conditions during the following three months were such as to prevent further conclusive aerial surveys.

At the beginning of 1917 the situation facing the Germans was grave. Whilst Britain, France and Russia were already in the process of rebuilding their armies, no fresh manpower was available. The creation of thirteen new divisions was under consideration but this was only possible by drawing on reserves and reducing existing establishments. Ludendorff knew that he could not match the strength of the Allies on the Western Front and therefore a major offensive in France or Belgium was out of the question. He assumed that an Allied attack was imminent and therefore his only option was to stand fast and await the effects of unrestricted submarine warfare on the Allies, which could well take another twelve months to manifest itself. Construction of the Hindenburg Line was well under way and, although originally seen as a rear defence system, it now became clear that the bulk of the troops were too worn out to withstand another Somme. Withdrawal to the Hindenburg Line presented a means of reducing the length of the

defence line by some twenty-five miles, at the same time saving thirteen or fourteen divisions. On 4 February the Kaiser gave his consent to *Operation Alberich*, a programme prepared by Crown Prince Rupprecht's Army Group for the systematic withdrawal to the Hindenburg Line. The name of the operation *Alberich* was derived from the Niebelung Saga, as was *Siegfried*. But whereas Siegfried was the hero, Alberich was the malicious dwarf which was in

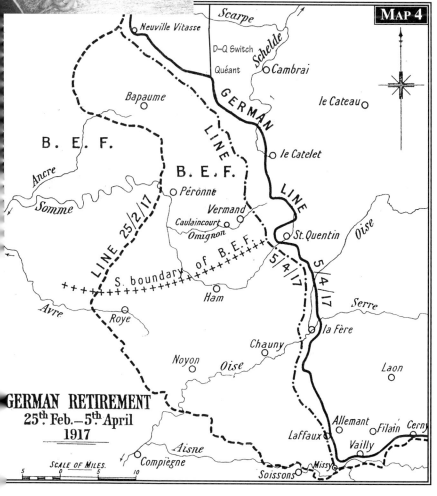

GERMAN RETIREMENT
25ᵗʰ Feb.—5ᵗʰ April
1917

many ways appropriate for what was to follow. The *Alberich* programme required 35 days for completion. The first 'Alberich Day' was 9 February and the last 15 March. The first 'Marching Day' was 16 March and the whole withdrawal was to be completed in two to four days. In the period between the first and last 'Alberich Days' the whole area to be evacuated was to be laid waste and made uninhabitable to the enemy. Trees were cut down, railways torn up, houses demolished, roads destroyed and junctions cratered. Wells were either filled in or polluted but not poisoned. Crown Prince Rupprecht objected to the degree of devastation, and indeed threatened to resign over it, but was overruled by Hindenburg.

As recorded by General Gough:

'On the 24th February the first definite signs of the Germans' retirement came to our notice. Patrols found front trenches deserted all along the front. Orders were issued immediately from the Army for strong patrols, backed up by advanced guards, to be pushed forward as far as possible.

By the 25th we had advanced 2,000 yards, and the villages of Warlencourt, Pys, Irles, Miraumont and Serre fell into our hands.

By the end of February the Australians were within 2,000 yards of the outskirts of Bapaume and the large villages of Puisieux and Gommecourt had been occupied.

The enemy's rear-guards, however, now stood firm for some time. There were two powerfully-constructed and quite undamaged hostile lines of entrenchments facing us, the first known as the Grévillers line, stretching roughly from the village of Bucquoy on the north by Achiet-le-Petit, Loupart Wood and the village of Tilloy; the other line, from 2,000 to 3,000 yards behind it, stretched across the villages of Ablainville, Bihucourt, and the western outskirts of Bapaume.

Here the German rear-guards held us till the 10th March.' [1]

By 18 March, the Australians had occupied Bapaume, but further advance was held up to enable engineers, aided by every available man, to embark on a programme of reconstruction to restore communications destroyed as part of *Operation Alberich*. In addition, the Germans had left behind delayed-action mines and booby-traps, carefully placed, and hidden, to cause maximum losses and harassment. The Town Hall at Bapaume was blown up by a large mine several days after it had been re-occupied, killing several soldiers and the Député for Bapaume, who had returned post haste from Paris, where he had resided since the commencement of the war.

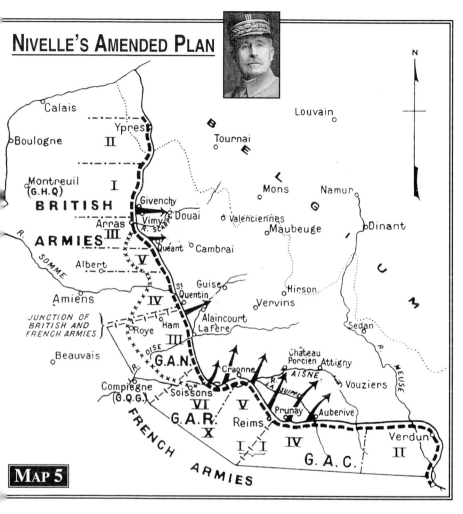

NIVELLE'S AMENDED PLAN

MAP 5

As a consequence of the German withdrawal, General Nivelle was forced to modify his plans. The offensive was now to commence with the British attacks on the Arras front to be followed two days later by the attack at St. Quentin by the French Third Army (G.A.N.). The main French attack by the Sixth, Fifth and Tenth Armies (G.A.R.), by now universally referred to as the 'Groupe des Armées de Rupture', was to follow after a further two days. One day later still, the final attack would be launched by the French Fourth Army (G.A.C.) **(See map 5)**. In the interim, however, the French Government had fallen, and Nivelle had lost the support of the Prime Minister who had selected him.

Briand was replaced as Prime Minister by Alexandre Ribot, with a new Minister of War, Paul Panlevé, who mistrusted Nivelle.

On 3 April, Nivelle was cross-questioned by the Comité de Guerre but given leave to proceed with his plans. Yet this was not to be the final word. On hearing of the decision taken by the Comité, Colonel Messimy, Minister of War in 1914, and now commanding a division, sent a strongly-worded memorandum to the War Committee criticising Nivelle's intentions. In a final attempt to resolve the dilemma, a formal Council of War was called for 6 April attended by the President of the Republic, Ramon Poincaré. After listening to criticism from his generals, Nivelle offered to resign, but the political repercussions of his removal would have been too great. He was finally given leave to proceed, on the understanding that, if no breakthrough was obtained in two days, the action would be broken off.

The bad weather which had earlier prevented aerial observation of the Hindenburg Line, deteriorated further during January and February 1917. If Joffre's original plan had been adhered to, it is doubtful whether an offensive in February would have been possible given the state of the ground. The adverse conditions continued into March and April. Nivelle's plans, which were well known to the Germans, through captured documents and poor security in Paris, were delayed until 9 April. Even then, the British attack at Arras opened in a snow storm. The bad visibility, which hindered the artillery observers and aerial reconnaissance, led to two further postponements on the part of the French. The attack by the G.A.R. was eventually launched on 16 April followed by that of the G.A.C. on 17 April. Nivelle's ambitions plans were not fulfilled and he in turn was 'limogé' on 15 May, to be replaced as Commander-in-Chief by Henri Pétain.

Bibliography

1. *The Fifth Army General.* Sir Hubert Gough. Hodder & Stoughton 1931.

Chapter Two

FIRST BATTLE OF BULLECOURT

By mid-March 1917, after the transfer of II and XIII Corps to strengthen other Armies, General Sir Hubert Gough's Fifth Army consisted of only two Corps: V Corps (Lieutenant-General Sir Edward Fanshawe) and I Anzac Corps (Lieutenant-General Sir William Birdwood). As a result of the German retreat, the Fifth Army's original role was no longer relevant, but if the attack at Arras by the Third Army was successful, then it would sweep across the new front held by the Fifth Army e.g. the right of the German line in front of the Arras sector. A simultaneous attack by General Gough would threaten the enemy's flank and rear, while he was already engaged in repelling a major attack. If the Fifth Army could move up to face the Hindenburg Line and be provided with sufficient artillery fire power to remove the belts of wire, then such an attack could be feasible. Intent on at least aiding the Third Army by bombarding the Hindenburg Line, Gough ordered up artillery from II Corps and the I Anzac Corps. Unfortunately, that of I Anzac Corps had to be brought up via Bapaume, the road to which was still far from perfect. The engineers had managed to render the road suitable for light vehicle and horse-drawn traffic, but with only a narrow strip paved for heavier traffic. The large artillery pieces were towed by tracked vehicles and hold-ups were common-place. Bean describes the scene, quoting from the diary of an unnamed Australian:

General Sir Hubert Gough

Lt-Gen Sir William Birdwood

Lt-Gen Sir Sir Edward Fanshawe

> '*After passing the last big crater near Le Sars (about 6.30 p.m.) we ran into a block. It had been half-raining and half-snowing, and the road was slush. A big lorry had stuck and its*

wheels dug in. Two light cars had tried to pass it and each stuck in the soft roadside. A tractor-caterpillar bringing down a big gun came down and pulled the lorry out, and the two cars, and then on the way back got stuck itself. Another caterpillar with a gun broke down on the other side of the road a few yards from him. A signal lorry broke down further up. An officer of the 2nd Divisional Headquarters and I worked for three hours getting the traffic gradually along.' [1]

This and similar hold-ups resulted in it taking nearly a week for the bulk of the artillery to reach Bapaume. Some batteries were able to open fire on parts of Bullecourt village on 20 March, but the bombardment proper did not commence until 4 April, and then gradually built up as batteries moved into the areas in front of the enemy positions. Supplies of ammunition were also delayed. These had to be brought up by train using the railway line into Achiet-le-Grand, which was not fully operational until 28 March.

In readiness for a possible attack, Gough ordered, on 21 March, that following the clearance of the enemy from the villages of Noreuil, Ecoust and Lagnicourt, which in the event took until 2 April, preparations should begin for assaulting the Hindenburg Line. On the following day, he received orders from GHQ instructing him to prepare to deliver an attack on the front between Quéant and Ecoust, in

Transport rounding the mine crater in the Albert-Bapaume road at Le Sars. About 19 March 1917. IWM E(AUS) 398

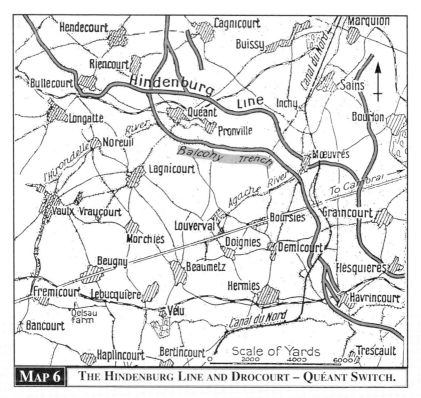

| MAP 6 | THE HINDENBURG LINE AND DROCOURT – QUÉANT SWITCH. |

conjunction with the operations of the Third Army. At the same time the Fifth Army was instructed to lend assistance, in artillery, to the right of the Third Army attack, as might be possible in view of the difficulties of bringing forward heavy and siege batteries.

Gough was eager to support General Allenby's Third Army operation. At a conference at GHQ on 24 March, Gough stated his

opinion that the Germans were using the Hindenburg Line merely as a rear-guard position, but that he would be ready to attack with two divisions, on a 3,000 - 4,000 yard front by 8 April. He was tempted to include Quéant in the attack as the village was the junction of the Hindenburg Line and the Drocourt-Quéant Switch but this would have presented a problem. From Quéant southward the second trench system would mean that the attackers would have had to break through

Mine crater in Bapaume 22 March 1917. IWM Q36251

four lines of trenches **(See map 6)**. Haig, however, decided that Gough's task should only involve the capture of a section of the Hindenburg Line and that exploitation should be down to the 4th Cavalry Division. In an attempt to ensure that Gough was able to attain the breakthrough, Haig allocated twelve tanks to the Fifth Army.

For once, Gough did not show his usual impatience. He assured his

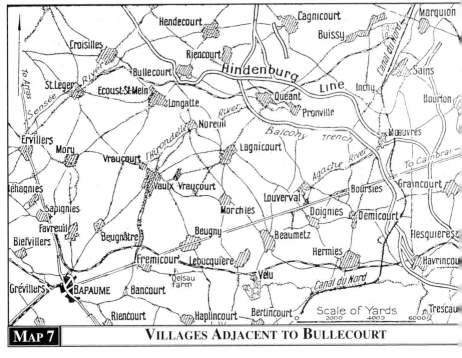

MAP 7   **VILLAGES ADJACENT TO BULLECOURT**

Corps commanders that no attack would be carried out until he was certain that the preparations had been thoroughly completed. It was not until 5 April that Australian troops entered the ground in the vicinity of the railway embankment, which was about 1,000 yards from the positions to be attacked. A similar situation faced the British on V Corps front, who were to attack on the other side of Bullecourt. Gough also modified the plans to include, in the objectives, two villages, Riencourt-les-Cagnicourt (Riencourt) and Hendecourt-les-Cagnicourt (Hendecourt), half a mile and one mile respectively beyond the Hindenburg Line **(See map 7)**.

It became clear that the artillery was not producing the results intended. Consequent upon the siting of the Hindenburg defences, on the reverse slope, out of sight of artillery observers, difficulty was being experienced in controlling the accuracy of the barrage. Aerial

The ground, to the left of Central Road, over which the Australians had to pass to reach the Hindenburg Line.

DIGGER MEMORIAL   CENTRAL ROAD

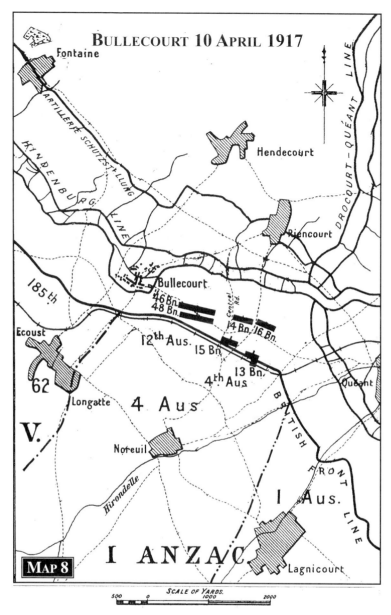

BULLECOURT 10 APRIL 1917

Fontaine
HINDENBURG LINE
ARTILLERIE-SCHÜTZSTELLUNG
Hendecourt
DROCOURT – QUÉANT LINE
Riencourt
185th
Bullecourt
46 Bn.
48 Bn.
Central Rd.
14 Bn. 16 Bn.
Ecoust
12th Aus. 15 Bn.
13 Bn.
4th Aus.
Quéant
62
Longatte
4 Aus
BRITISH
V.
Noreuil
FRONT
Hirondelle
I Aus.
LINE
MAP 8
I ANZAC
Lagnicourt
SCALE OF YARDS.
500 0 1000 2000

photography, confirmed by the reports of a night patrol, on 7 April, showed that the wire had not been sufficiently cut and the attack was postponed until at least 12 April.

On Easter Monday, 9 April 1917, the Battle of Arras opened, with attacks on Vimy Ridge by the First Army and at Arras by the Third Army. As the day progressed reports of successes reached the Fifth Army HQ. In the afternoon a reassessment of the part to be played by the tanks on the Fifth Army front led to Gough issuing orders that the attack should take place next day. The role of the tanks will be looked at, in detail, later in the chapter. By 11.00 p.m. it was clear that the breakthrough on the left of the Fifth Army had not been achieved, and that the use of the cavalry by the Third Army was, therefore, out of the question. Following consultations between Sir William Birdwood and Neill Malcolm, Gough's Chief of Staff, the decision to attack was confirmed, as was the proposal to exploit any breakthrough on the Fifth Army front by the 4th Cavalry Division. This division would now be assisting VII Corps.

By the time of the attack on 10 April, the British Fifth Army front line ran in front of Ecoust, Longatte, Noreuil and Lagnicourt The

Artillery observers registering the Australian batteries' shots on the wire of the Hindenburg Line. IWM E(Aus) 603

BULLECOURT VILLAGE

boundary between Gough's two corps lay through the eastern edge of
Longatte and on a line towards Bullecourt village. On the left, V Corps
sector, the line was held by the 62nd (West Riding) Division. On the
right, the I Anzac, had the 4th Division on the left and the 1st Division
on the right, **(See map 8)**. The tanks were to operate with the
Australian 4th Division. The ground in front of Bullecourt consisted of
a succession of depressions and spurs which ran directly towards the
enemy's lines, with little intervening cover. Orders for the attack were
issued during the remainder of the day. The Australian 4th Division
only received their final orders at 12.25 a.m. on 10 April leaving some

CENTRAL ROAD →

The Railway Embankment and Central Road. Dugouts, used as headquarters, were set into the side of the embankment for safety.

four hours for preparation, as zero hour was set for 4.30 a.m. At 1.00 a.m. Bullecourt was drenched with poison gas, using a new weapon, the Livens projector (See chapter 7).

The introduction of the tanks

The tank was developed during 1915, mainly at the instigation of, and under pressure from, two men: Winston Churchill, First Lord of the Admiralty; and Colonel Ernest Swinton. The first tank to have the characteristic rhomboid shape was successfully demonstrated at Hatfield Park, the home of Lord Salisbury, on the 2 February 1916, in the presence of a distinguished company which included Lord Kitchener, Sir William Robertson, David Lloyd George, Minister of Munitions and Arthur Balfour who had replaced Winston Churchill as First Lord of the Admiralty. An order for one hundred tanks was placed

British tanks moving up to the line before the Battle of Arras. Tank Museum

RECENTLY REPLANTED MORY COPSE

DEPRESSION IN WHICH TANKS WERE CONCEALED

Site of Mory copse where the tanks were hidden before the attack on 11 April 1917.

shortly afterwards, which was soon increased to one hundred and fifty.

Two types of Mark I tank were produced, the 'male' and the 'female'; the major difference between them was the design of the sponsons. The 'male' was designed to carry two six-pounder guns, mounted one on each side and four machine guns. It was intended that the 'male' would cross wire and trenches. The 'female' was to cope with infantry at close quarters and carried five machine guns, with a large arc of fire. The difference resulted in a small weight differential, the 'male' weighed twenty-eight tons whereas the 'female' weighed twenty-seven tons. In other respects they were identical. Both Mark I tanks were fitted with two heavy wheels at the rear, primarily designed as an aid to steering. In the field, they were found to be unreliable and were soon abandoned. The casing of both tanks was armour plating, held in place by rivets.

The tanks started to arrive in France in June 1916 and six companies, 'A' to 'F', were recruited to crew them. The name given to the new unit was 'the Heavy Section, Machine Gun Corps' but this was changed a few months later to 'the Heavy Branch, Machine Gun Corps.'

Machine Gun Corps.'

The tanks made their first appearance on the battlefield on 15 September 1916. Following the failure of the projected breakthrough on the Somme, Sir Douglas Haig had pressed for tanks to be made available as soon as possible. The debate still continues as to whether their use in 1916, when only limited numbers were available, was justified. Would it have been better to wait until 1917, when they could have been introduced en masse, whilst retaining the element of surprise?

Haig's confidence in the tank was not dented by their performance in the Battle of Flers-Courcelette. He requested that the rate of production of tanks be accelerated, and that the training programme for crews expanded. In November 1916, at the same time as the name change, the decision was made to abandon the company system in favour of battalions. The First Tank Brigade or as it was called at the time, the First Battalion of the Heavy Branch, Machine Gun Corps, was formed from the nucleus provided by the old 'A', 'B' 'C' and 'D' Companies of tanks which had formed the fighting unit in France. At the close of the Somme battle, these four companies were withdrawn for training and reconstruction. On 1 February 1917 two tank battalions were formed from the old 'C' and 'D' Companies and brigaded under the command of Colonel C.D'A.B.S. Baker-Carr. The two battalions were 'C' Battalion, formed from the old 'C' Company, and commanded by Lieutenant-Colonel Charrington and 'D' Battalion, formed from the old 'D' Company, and commanded by Lieutenant-Colonel J. Hardress Lloyd.

The Battle of Arras saw the entry of the First Battalion as a fighting unit. A total of sixty tanks were allocated, twenty-eight to 'C' Battalion and thirty-two to 'D' Battalion. All these tanks were either Mark I or Mark II. No Mark IV tanks were yet available. However, some small changes had been effected since the previous autumn. The main armament in the 'male' tank remained the six-pounder but the machine guns were changed to Lewis guns. The 'female' also now carried Lewis, instead of Vickers and Hotchkiss, machine guns. Although the Lewis gun was an excellent infantry weapon, it did not function well in tanks.

British tanks April 1917. Tank Museum

The tanks allocated to the Fifth Army belonged to No. 11 Company 'D' Battalion (H.B.M.G.C.). All of these were Mark II tanks, which were training models taken over to France as an emergency measure. They were not intended to be used in battle, so no armour plating was fitted to their exterior! Just as Gough experienced difficulties in getting artillery and ammunition up to the front, so the tank commanders suffered getting their tanks to their base at Mory Copse, three miles from Ecoust.

'My tanks arrived at Achiet-le-Grand just after dawn on 1 April. We had taken them from the central workshops at Erin, and had drawn there a vast variety of equipment. The tanks had been driven on to the train by an Engineer officer. The railway journey was delayed as usual, and the usual expert - this time a doctor - had walked along the train, when shunted at Doullens, and had pointed out to his companion the 'new monster tanks.'

In the morning we hauled off the sponson-trolleys, but we thought it wiser to wait until dusk before we detrained the tanks.

Tanks travel on flat trucks, such as are employed to carry rails. They are driven on and off the train under their own power, but this performance requires care, skill and experience. A Mk. I or Mk. IV tank is not easy to steer, while the space between the edge of the track and the edge of the truck is alarmingly small. With two exceptions, my officers had neither experience nor skill.

It was an anxious time - not only for the company commander. The office of the R.T.O., at the edge of the ramp, was narrowly missed on two occasions. Very slowly and with infinite care the tanks were persuaded to leave the train and move down the road to the tankodrome we had selected. Then it began first to sleet then to snow, while an icy wind rose, until a blizzard was lashing our faces.

The Sunken Road occupied by Australian troops, after Captain Jacka's reconnaissance, looking west.

The Sunken Road occupied by Australian troops, after Captain Jacka's reconnaissance, looking east.

In the old Mk. I. tank it was necessary to detach the sponsons, or armoured 'bow-windows' on either side before the tank could be moved by rail. This was no easy matter. The tank was driven into two shallow trenches. A stout four-wheeled trolley was run alongside, and a sort of crane was fitted, to which slings were secured. The sponson was girt about with these slings, the bolts which secured the sponson to the body of the tank were taken out, and the sponson lowered on to the trolley.

My men, of whom the majority were inexperienced, carried out the reverse process on a dark night in a blizzard. Their fingers were so blue with cold that they could scarcely handle their tools. The climax was reached when they discovered that we should be compelled to drill new holes in several of the sponsons, because in certain cases the holes in the sponsons did not correspond with the holes in the tanks.

If the men had a harder night's work, they certainly never worked better. Half the tanks fitted their sponsons and reached Behagnies at dawn. The remainder, less one lame duck, were hidden in Achiet-le-Grand until darkness once more allowed them to move.'[2]

By dawn on 6 April the eleven tanks were safely camouflaged in an old quarry at Mory Copse. It was still the intention that the tanks should used in pairs across the front, a technique which did not find favour with tank officers. The reassessment of the role of the tanks (already referred to) followed a meeting of General Gough with Colonel Hardress Lloyd and Major W.H.L. Watson, of the 1st Tank Battalion. Watson had already convinced Hardress Lloyd that, given the difficulties being experienced by the artillery, a surprise concentration might be better than the proposed format. His proposal required the tanks to attack on a restricted front, the artillery not opening fire until the tanks had passed through the wire. As stated in the Official History:

> 'Under the new scheme the attack was to be carried out on a frontage of about 1,500 yards against the re-entrant in the Hindenburg Line between Quéant and Bullecourt by the 4th Australian Division alone. The tanks were to line up in front of the infantry and penetrate the wire ahead of them. As soon as the Hindenburg Line had been taken four tanks were to swing westward into Bullecourt, followed by an Australian battalion, and to clear the village. The 62nd Division was then to push through to its original objective of Hendecourt, while the Australian right assisted by four tanks advanced on Riencourt.'[3]

The Australian 4th Division

The Australian 4th Division held the line on the left of the Anzac front. The commanding officer of the division, Major-General W. Holmes, decided to use two brigades in the attack. The 12th Brigade, on the left, would use two battalions, the 46th to assault and capture the Hindenburg Line, and the 48th, to follow the tanks into Bullecourt. The 4th Brigade, on the right, would employ all four battalions, as it had as an additional objective, the village of Riencourt. The 14th Battalion on the brigade's left, and the 16th Battalion on its right, would lead, and be followed by the 15th Battalion and 13th Battalion respectively. Between the two brigades, there was a gap, of about 400 yards. This gap, which lay at the bottom of a depression, followed the line of Central Road **(See map 9)**. It was considered that the area would be a 'deadly channel for the enemy's machine gun fire.' As stated in the Official History:

> 'It was hoped that the tanks would deal with the defences here, and that the brigades would afterwards be able to close the gap by extending their inner flanks.'[4]

On the night of the 7 April, the 4th Division had four battalions, the 48th, 46th, the 16th and the 14th in the line. They were deployed, from left to right, along the embankment of the railway, which ran from

Boisleux, in the west, to Marquion, in the east, at right angles to the direction of the attack. During the night, the Intelligence Officer of the 14th Battalion, Captain Albert Jacka VC MC, prowled forward into No Man's Land and discovered that a sunken track, which ran from Quéant to Bullecourt, parallel with the railway but some 300 yards closer to the enemy lines, was unoccupied. At dusk on the following evening, the 14th and 16th Battalions advanced, and occupied this track. To the left, on the other side of Central Road, the 46th Battalion also occupied the track, leaving the 48th Battalion in previously-dug assembly trenches, in front of the railway line. When the final orders were received for the attack, Brigadier-General C.H. Brand, commanding

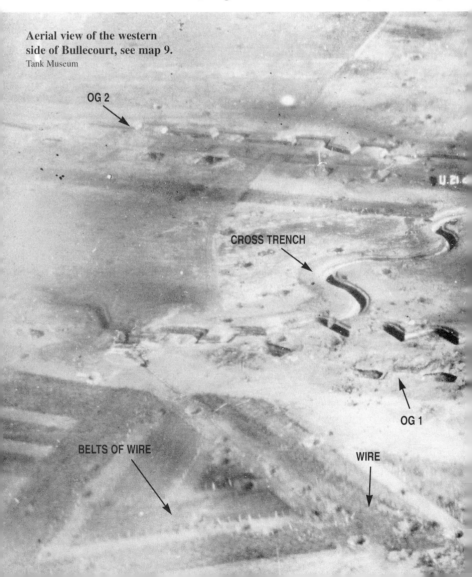

Aerial view of the western side of Bullecourt, see map 9.
Tank Museum

OG 2

CROSS TRENCH

OG 1

BELTS OF WIRE

WIRE

the 4th Brigade, ordered his two remaining battalions, the 13th and 15th, forward from their positions in Favreuil, near Bapaume. At 10 p.m., they left to take up positions behind the 14th and 16th Battalions.

As part of the preparation before the attack, Gough ordered reconnaissance to be carried out to ascertain the state of the enemy wire and trenches. An officer's patrol, consisting of Captain A. Jacka, 14th Battalion, and Lieutenants H. Bradley and F. Wadge, 6th Battalion, went out just after dusk on the 9th, to examine, and report on, the state of the defences opposite the 4th Brigade. They penetrated inside the German wire and concluded that 'it was useless to attack the Hindenburg Line without artillery support.' They also stated that the

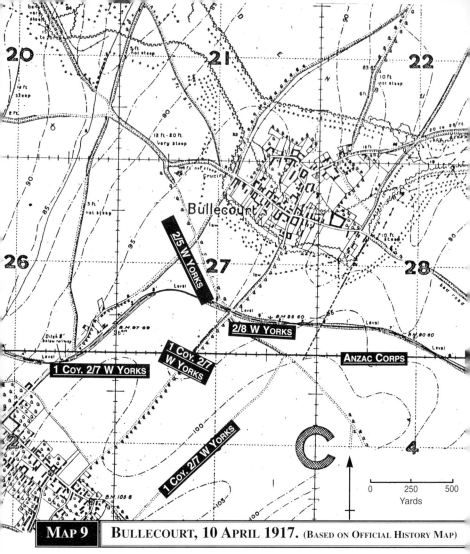

MAP 9 | **BULLECOURT, 10 APRIL 1917.** (BASED ON OFFICIAL HISTORY MAP)

enemy was still present in large numbers in the Hindenburg Line. Similar reports were sent back by patrols on the 12th Brigade front. There were some large gaps in the wire, but in front of Bullecourt village the wire was still very thick and largely uncut.

Following the reports on the state of the wire, and less favourable reports on the progress of the Third Army, General Birdwood telephoned Neill Malcolm, Gough's Chief of Staff, at 11.00 p.m. expressing concern over the proposed attack. As already noted a rapid response was received from General Gough insisting that the attack went forward as planned. He later told Major-General C.B. White, Birdwood's Chief of Staff, that the failure on the Third Army front

42

made it all the more important that the Fifth Army attack.

At 2.15 a.m. Jacka and Bradley again went out into No Man's Land. Their task was to lay tapes for the assaulting troops. The tapes laid, they set off to return to their own lines when two Germans were seen approaching the tapes. Bean relates what followed.

'Seeing that they would probably detect the tapes, and must therefore on no account be allowed to return, Jacka at once decided to cut them off. For assistance he went back to the position of an advanced sentry group, but finding it withdrawn, hurried to the main line, secured the help of a Lewis gunner, and with him worked round behind the two Germans, now almost on the tapes. ...One who carried a cane, was evidently an officer, and the other, who had a rifle, his orderly. Jacka, now at five yards distance, aimed his revolver at the officer's head and, when the trigger merely clicked, rushed in and seized him. He officer let fall his cane, the orderly threw down his rifle, Jacka captured the two, and began driving them towards the Australian line.'[5]

The captured officer, of the III/124th (Württemberg) Infantry Regiment, when subsequently interrogated by Colonel J.H. Peck, commanding the 14th Battalion, complained of his treatment by Jacka, to which Peck replied that 'as he was captured by Jacka he was lucky to be alive'

The artillery fire was to continue as normal until 4.30 a.m., but at that time a heavy barrage would be directed on to both flanks. The tanks would advance, but the infantry would not follow until the tanks were in the Hindenburg Line. They would display signal discs to bring the infantry forward. At 2.30 a.m., the foremost battalions moved up to the starting lines and by 4.15 a.m., all units were in their allotted positions, including the supporting 13th and 15th Battalions along the railway embankment. During the night, the weather had deteriorated with rain turning to sleet and finally to snow. The men lying out in the snow-covered ground waited for the sound of the tanks approaching down the Noreuil valley.

Following Gough's decision to attack within twenty-four hours, Major Watson rushed back to his HQ at Behagnies and despatched orders to Mory Copse. By 8.00 p.m. the tanks were on the move from the copse. Watson then drove to the HQ of the Australian 4th Division to await their arrival. Unfortunately, soon after the tanks set out, the snow became so hard that all landmarks were blotted out. The drivers even had difficulty seeing the officers, who were leading their tanks on foot. They never actually got lost, but by the time they arrived in the valley running down from Vaulx-Vraucourt to Noreuil, they were so tired and so late, that it was impossible for them to reach the starting point on time. The attack had already been delayed once, but now the decision was made to abandon it altogether and to recall the Australians from their exposed positions in the snow-covered fields. They streamed back, 'like a crowd leaving a test match' but just as it seemed that they must be seen by the enemy, in the early morning light, snow started again and quickly became a blizzard. The withdrawal was achieved almost without casualties, except on the 48th Battalion front where Major B.B. Leane was killed. He was second-in-command to his brother, the battalion commander. This battalion was affectionately know as the 'Joan of Arc Battalion' as it contained so many members of the Leane family, that it was 'Made of All-Leanes.' Major Leane is buried in Quéant Road Cemetery, Buissy.

Extract from a memoir written by Private Leslie Robert Pezet No. 3416 15th Battalion AIF. Written on board the Troopship 'Derbyshire' en route for Australia, 1919.

Bapaume

'At dusk Fritz shells heavily and we have to go. We get on our way and we get all reckless and hurry over the ridge, twenty of us all told. Then for two hundred yards we crawl on hands and knees through mud and slush, wishing the Germans to hell with the war. After all our trouble, we reach the position and find only two dead men, killed before the other lads evacuated. We bury these men and wait for the 9th Battalion to come and relieve us. They were four and a half hours late.

On the evening of 10th April we are ordered a good issue of rum and a big dinner, and all to be ready at nine o'clock to march to the line, carrying full packs, blankets, pick and shovel, 200 rounds of ammunition, and a sandbag of canteen stuff for ourselves. We get to the sunken road and dump packs and rations. When the attack is finished, carriers will bring these along to the fighters. We are formed in line, bayonets fixed, waiting for the order to come from the right to charge over a distance of 1200 yards. Daybreak upon us, the order comes to retire at the double. Everyone is sick at heart, having made up our minds to go into it and get it over and the German guns are quiet and no machine gun fire. We are mad. We start to retire and the Huns see us. Machine gun and artillery fire are terrible. A *snow storm comes and the Huns scatter their fire and they cannot see us, and we dodge it with very few men not to answer Roll Call on our return. We are told that the tanks failed, being knocked out. We reach our positions one by one. All day men come in and fall down, not lying down.'*

The 62nd (West Riding) Division

On the night of 4/5 April, the 185th Brigade took over the line from the 22nd Brigade, 7th Division. The front line held by the 62nd Division, ran from the Bullecourt-Longatte road, thence in a north-westerly direction to the bank of the River Sensée. The flanking divisions were, on the right, the 4th Australian and on the left, the British 21st. In front of the main defence line was an outpost line, and behind the former, in support, a line of companies and platoons, at points varying from five hundred to two thousand yards in the rear of the railway. The village of Bullecourt lay in a salient, with a strong trench and wire system around three sides. Another trench ran through the village and finally another wire and trench system ran behind it, to the north **(See map 9)**. The wire was very dense and enemy machine guns, expertly positioned, were able to fire along its length. At this time, the village had not been destroyed but, just in front of the enemy's wire two mines had been exploded. These caused two large craters, one in the road from Bullecourt to Ecoust and the other in the road from Bullecourt to Longatte.

The 62nd
Division

By the evening of 5 April, three battalions of the Division were in the front line. They were, from right to left, the 2/7, the 2/8 and 2/5 West Yorkshires, dispersed in depth, in the outpost line, the main line and the support line.

On 8 April the commander of V Corps had issued Operation Order No. 134, which stated:

> *'Although an attack on big scale will not be made on the 10th instant, the following instructions are issued with regard to the action to be taken by the artillery and infantry. Preparations will be made to carry these out on the 10th instant or at any time after that date, <u>on receipt of orders from Corps H.Q.</u>*
>
> *(a) A bombardment and barrage will commence at zero hour as for the big attack up to the first objective only. Strong patrols of the 62nd Division will be sent forward close under the barrage, who will endeavour to occupy the line of the first objective.'*

Although no such order was issued, in the activity following upon

Gough's order for the attack within twenty-four hours, two messages were sent to the 62nd Division: the first dealing with the advance of patrols, and the second stating that zero hour had been set for 4.30 a.m. These messages were interpreted as being the orders referred to in the underlined section of Operation Order No. 134. They were also informed that tanks and the Australian Brigade on the right of the 2/7 West Yorks. were to co-operate.

Strong patrols, which were made up from the three West Yorkshire battalions, went forward at 4.35 a.m. Within ten minutes the 2/7 West Yorkshire had passed through the first belt of wire. Five minutes later, disaster struck. The enemy machine guns opened fire and cut the patrols to pieces. On the left of the 2/8 West Yorkshire, the foremost parties of the 2/5 West Yorkshire were so badly cut up that the following ones were not despatched. At 5.10 a.m., with no sign of the supporting Australians or of the tanks, the patrols started to withdraw. Unlike the withdrawal by the Australians, this was not achieved without serious loss. A total of 162 casualties was recorded, the majority being in the 2/7 West Yorkshires. This battalion reported one officer wounded, together with nineteen other ranks killed, seventy-two wounded and nineteen missing.

The Australians informed the division that the tanks had not arrived and that consequently the attack was postponed at 4.55 a.m., twenty-five minutes after zero hour. By this time, the patrols had been despatched and were in trouble. Liaison between the Australian and the British was at fault, but it is arguable whether this was the result of decisions taken higher up in the chain of command. Gough's order, to attack within twenty-four hours, left too little time for proper staff work to be carried out.

At noon on 10 April, Gough called a meeting of all his senior commanders together with their chiefs of staff. He informed those present that the Third Army was that day to renew its attempt to force a passage through the German lines. To aid this operation, he planned to re-schedule the morning's aborted attack, for 4.30 a.m. the following day, 11 April. Alterations to the plan were made as the day progressed, but although the final details were more considered, the time for implementation was again limited. In its final form the scheme required that:

1. The infantry was no longer to await a signal from the tanks, but follow after a fifteen minute delay.
2. Diagrams of the proposed position and role of each tank be issued.

3. To help the tanks effect surprise, there would be no creeping barrage for the infantry or preliminary bombardment of the objective. Bullecourt itself would be drenched in gas.
4. The general bombardment would continue all night but would cease on Bullecourt at 5.00 a.m., and on Riencourt at 5.15 a.m., to permit entry into each village. When the tanks reached the Hindenburg Line, the field artillery would set up a barrage on both flanks.
5. The 62nd Division would only move forward after the tanks and Anzac troops had entered Bullecourt.

The action of the tanks on 11 April

> 'Here we encounter a veritable legend and one of the most curious of the war.'[6]

The plan, as issued, required the twelve tanks of D Battalion to be positioned as shown **(See map 10)**, six in front of each brigade. The four in the centre would progress through the depression, to attack the centre portion of the defences not attacked by the infantry. The four on

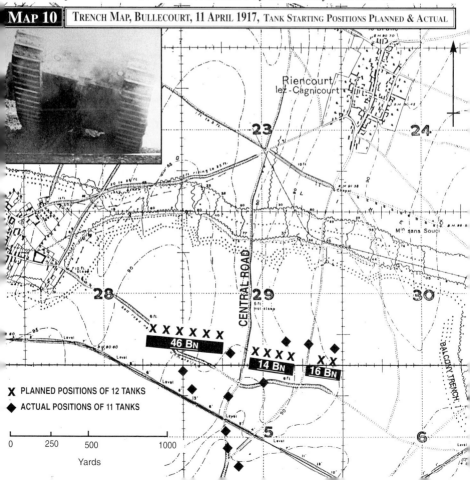

MAP 10 | TRENCH MAP, BULLECOURT, 11 APRIL 1917, TANK STARTING POSITIONS PLANNED & ACTUAL

X PLANNED POSITIONS OF 12 TANKS
◆ ACTUAL POSITIONS OF 11 TANKS

0   250   500   1000
                Yards

the flanks would turn outwards, as they reached respectively, the first and second lines of the Hindenburg Line. Those on the right would crush the wire of the two lines and then attempt to do the same to the wire in front of the Balkon-Stellung (Balcony Trench) near Quéant, before returning to Noreuil. The two on the left, would combine with two next to them to take Bullecourt. They would then link up with the two, to their right, to lead the 62nd Division from Bullecourt to Hendecourt. In the event, there were only eleven tanks available, one was still out of action in Achiet-le-Grand, so the number designated to attack the central area of wire was reduced to three. After the postponement of the earlier attack, the tanks were parked nearby in Noreuil valley. This should have meant that no problems would be encountered in getting them into position on time, but this proved to be very far from the truth. The officer given responsibility for getting the tanks into their starting lines was Captain Jacka. He succeeded with the first, by 3.20 a.m., but when he checked with the tank commander that fifteen minutes was sufficient time for his tank to reach the wire, he was horrified to be told that at least 30 minutes were necessary. In an effort to save the 14th and 16th Battalions from facing uncut wire, he hurried back to the battalion headquarters, on the side of the railway,

General Birdwood with Captain Albert Jacka, VC, MC, after presenting him with a Bar to the MC, for bravery during the fighting for Bullecourt.
IWM E(AUS) 450

to report the situation to the respective commanding officers, Colonels Peck and Drake Brockman. They, in turn, requested from General Holmes, an earlier start for the tanks but were told that no alterations in the plans were possible.

When Jacka returned to Central Road, he found that two more tanks had arrived. These he escorted forward, into line with the first, but separated, one from another by about a hundred yards. The three were 150 yards in front of the infantry. A fourth tank, one that was to take a position on the far right, had broken down. Another, one of the three destined for the central position, went astray, and got stuck in the sunken road. By zero hour, Jacka had still only got three of the tanks scheduled to operate with the 4th Brigade into their allotted positions. The remainder, and those allocated to the 12th Brigade, were in the positions shown **(See map 10)**.

Once zero hour arrived and the tanks moved forward, the reports of what happened are, to say the least, at variance. The report filed in the War Diary states that all the tanks arrived on the front line at 4.45 a.m. They proceeded to break lanes into the wire, allowing the infantry through. This lead to the capture of both front and support trenches. It then goes on to detail the actions and fates of some of the tanks:

'Two tanks turned eastwards and broke down the wire, working eastwards.

Four tanks turned westwards and advanced against Bullecourt and of these four, only one reached Bullecourt, the other three each receiving direct hits from shells and put out of action.

This tank went into Bullecourt and cruised in the village shooting any Germans visible. The enemy fled in disorder. The infantry, apparently, were unable to keep close to this tank.

Two tanks assisted in the capture of Riencourt.

Two tanks led the infantry into Hendecourt.

All tanks were heavily shelled as, owing to the snow on the ground, they were conspicuous targets.

When retirement took place, damaged tanks had to be abandoned. The Lewis guns, where possible were salved. Two tanks were able to retire behind our lines. In this attack, eight tanks reached their first objective. Six tanks carried out their operations, as detailed after the capture of the first objective.'[7]

A manuscript 'War History of the 1st Tank Brigade', in the same file at The Public Record Office, also claims that Riencourt and Hendecourt were captured. This document is dated January 1919.

In his own account of the action, written in 1917, Major Watson describes in some detail the actions and outcomes. During the morning, he moved outside the village (Noreuil) to collect the men by the bank, where the tanks had sheltered, a few hours before. By this time the story of the operation was beginning to unfold.

'Skinner's tank failed on the embankment. The remainder crossed it successfully and lined up for the attack just before zero. By this time the shelling had become severe. The crews waited inside their tanks, wondering dully if they would be hit before they started. Already they were dead-tired, for they had had little sleep since their long painful trek the night before.

Suddenly our bombardment began - it was more of a bombardment than a barrage - and the tanks crawled away into the darkness, followed closely by little bunches of Australians.

He describes the fate of most of the tanks and includes a description of how one tank entered Bullecourt.

On the extreme right Morris and Puttock of Wyatt's section were met by tremendous machine gun fire at the wire of the Hindenburg Line. They swung to the right, as they had been ordered, and glided along the wire, sweeping the parapet with fire. By luck and good driving they returned to the railway. Morris passed a line to Skinner and towed him over the embankment. They both started for Bullecourt. Puttock pushed on back towards Noreuil. His clutch was slipping so badly that the tank would not move, and the shells were falling ominously near. He withdrew his crew from the tank into a trench, and a moment later the tank was hit and hit again.

Skinner, after his tank had been towed over the railway embankment by Morris, made straight for Bullecourt, thinking that as the battle had now been in progress for more that two hours the Australians must have fought their way down the trenches into the village. Immediately he entered the village machine guns played upon his tank, and several of his crew were slightly wounded by little flakes of metal that fly about inside a Mk. I tank when it is subjected to really concentrated machine gun fire. No Australians could be seen. Suddenly he came right to the edge of an enormous crater, and suddenly stopped. He tried to reverse but could not change gear. The tank was almost motionless. He held out for some time, and then the Germans brought up a gun and began to shell the tank. Against field guns in houses he was defenceless so long as his tank could not move.

His ammunition was nearly exhausted. There was no sign of the Australians or British troops. He decided, quite properly to withdraw. With great skill he evacuated his crew, taking his guns with him and the little ammunition that remained. Slowly and carefully they worked their way back, and reached the railway embankment without further casualty.' [8]

In the Australian Official History, Bean describes the line taken by each tank and identifies its final position. In his narrative, he had the advantage of access to German reports which were not available to the diarist or to Watson. Adopting Bean's numbering, *1* to *11*, each tank can be followed. He also refers to the two trench lines of the Hindenburg Line, as O.G.1 and O.G.2. (The use of this terminology was derived from the two lines of trenches, which the Australians had encountered at Pozières the previous year. The letters probably stood for 'Old German'). Between the two lines was a series of deep

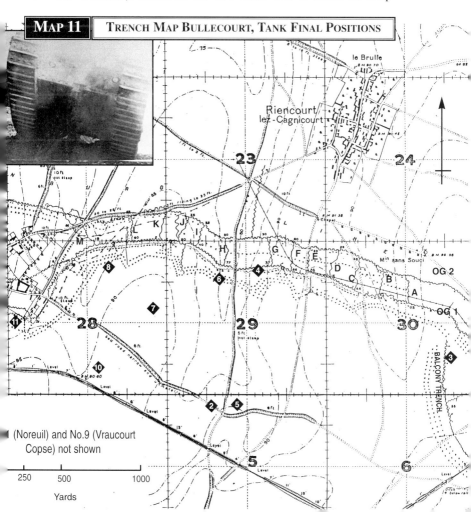

MAP 11   **TRENCH MAP BULLECOURT, TANK FINAL POSITIONS**

(Noreuil) and No.9 (Vraucourt Copse) not shown

250   500   1000

Yards

View, from the railway embankment, of the approximate final position of tank No. 10 on 11 April 1917.

communication or cross-trenches, identified by the letters A to M **(See map 11)**.

Numbers *1* and *2* (Lt. Morris & Lt. Puttock) were supposed to attack the front and support trenches respectively, cruise round the wire, and return to their start line. Neither reached the wire, and both were forced to retire. They were later disabled, *1* near Noreuil, and *2* near the railway. Numbers *3* and *4* (Lt. Davies and Lt. Clarkson) became separated. Davies' tank veered off to the right, where it crossed the wire, in front of Balcony Trench, about half a mile north-west of Quéant. It passed over the front trench, but was put out of action as it made its way towards the second. Clarkson's tank got through the wire, and reached O.G.2. It was put out of action as it he tried to recross O.G.1. Number *5* made little progress, almost immediately being hit by a shell which broke its track. Number *6* (Lt. Money) went forward in the central depression. It reached the wire but became enmeshed and was set on fire by a series of bomb attacks. Number *7* (Lt. Bernstein)

View, from the railway embankment, of the approximate final position of tank No. 11 on 11April 1917.

was abandoned after twice being hit near its starting point. The second hit, which decapitated the driver, left most of the crew stunned. The remaining four tanks were those allocated to the 12th Brigade. Numbers *8* and *9* arrived just before the brigade started, but were hit by shells early on. Number *8* was abandoned, in front of the wire, to the east of Bullecourt. Number *9* was brought out but became disabled near Vraucourt Copse. It was not until about 6.30 a.m. that tank number *10* (Lt. Birkett) reached the 48th Battalion HQ. The commanding officer, Colonel Leane, requested that the tank take out a troublesome machine gun in Bullecourt. The tank went forward, accomplished the task, but was later hit and disabled on the railway. The final tank, that of Lieutenant Skinner, was the one that entered Bullecourt and the story of its action there, given by Watson, is confirmed by Bean.

No mention is made of tanks reaching either Riencourt or Hendecourt.

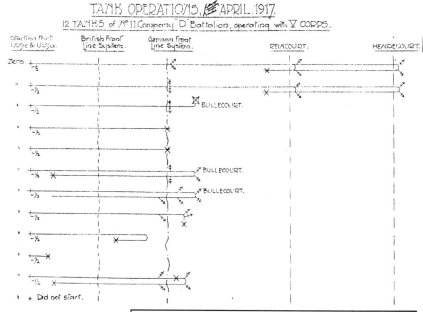

Diagram showing the fate of the tanks involved in 11 April, attack, at Bullecourt, as recorded in the unit war diary. Tank Museum

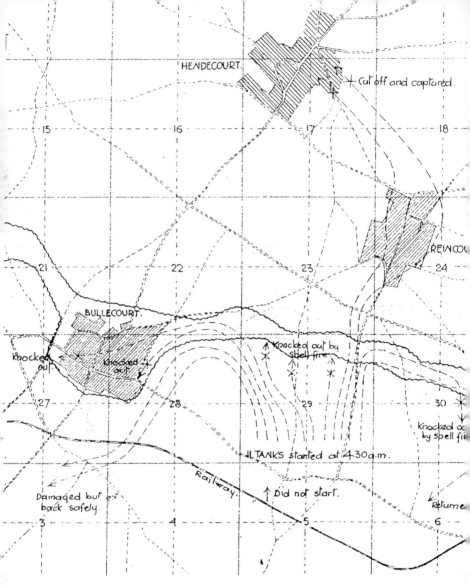

Bean sums up:

'So far as it was known on the spot, all the tanks - with the exception of that which entered Bullecourt - had fought their short fight in the area in rear of the Australian front line before 7 o'clock; their carcasses could be seen motionless, and in most cases burning, all over the battlefield. Of their crews - 103 officers and men - 52 were killed, wounded or missing. General Brand (4th Brigade) was at 7.21 informed by Jacka of their complete failure.'[9]

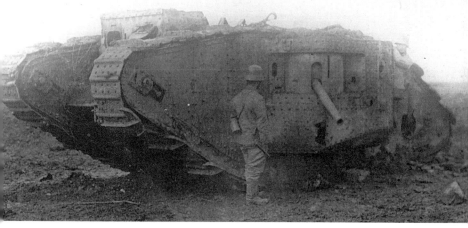

Two Germans inspect a disabled British tank.

Tank number D 799 was captured and displayed by the Germans. They were able to glean information about its construction and performance. In particular they discovered that the steel sides of tanks could be pierced by armour-piercing bullets. In future, all infantrymen and machine gunners, were supplied with 'K' or armour-piercing bullets. It must, however, be remembered that the tanks used were not armour-plated.

Copy of a letter sent to D Battalion H.B.M.G.C. following the operations on 11 April 19117. It was probably sent on 21st April. Tank Museum

```
O.C., "D" Battalion,          Fifth Army S.G. 67/27.
   H. B., M. G. Corps.            1st April, 1917.

        The Army Commander has read your report upon the
Tank Operations on the 11th April,    He is convinced
that the Tank Crews did everything that was possible to
ensure success,  and that the failure was due to no
fault of theirs.
        He will be glad if you will convey to Major WATSON
and all the Officers, N. C. Os, and men engaged, his
sincere thanks for their gallant efforts

             (Sd)  N. MALCOLM, Major General,
                General Staff.
```

Part of a tank from 1917, dug out of nearby ground, in the museum at Bullecourt.

Infantry actions on 11 April

It will be recalled, that the two Australian Brigades, the 4th and the 12th, were to attack with four battalions and two battalions respectively. For ease of understanding, each of the brigade attacks will be considered in turn **(See map 12)**.

The 4th Brigade

Following the cancellation of the attack on the 10th, the men of the 13th and 15th Battalions had trudged wearily back to their base at Favreuil, which they reached in the early afternoon. At 5.00 p.m. orders were received that the operation had only been delayed by twenty-four hours. At 9.00 p.m. they set off again, to rejoin the 16th and 14th

Battalions in the ground in front of the railway. At 4.45 a.m. next morning the brigade rose up and moved off. The 16th Battalion, led by Major Percy Black (See Chapter 5), passed over a small rise, overtook a tank and reached the wire in front of O.G.1, a distance of about seven hundred yards. Although not yet broken down by tanks, the wire was, in places, destroyed and the 16th were able to enter O.G.1. Leaving the leading wave to deal with the consolidation of their gains, Black led the second wave forward towards O.G.2. Unfortunately, between the two trenches was another belt of wire, almost untouched. Black managed to find a break in this wire but, as he pushed men forward, he was shot and killed. They fought their way on to O.G.2, where they were joined by men of the supporting 13th Battalion.

In the ground between Central Road and the track running from Noreuil to Riencourt, troops of the 14th Battalion, like those of the 16th, came under very heavy machine gun fire as they neared the first belt of wire. Once through this, they took further heavy casualties, crossing the stretch of ground between it and O.G.1. Once O.G.1 had been captured, the 15th came up, and together they moved on to O.G.2. It now remained for the 14th Battalion to make contact with the 12th Brigade on its left. To this end a bombing party, under Lieutenant W. Parsonage, set off to work its way westward down O.G.1. They managed to gain about one hundred yards before being stopped by a combination of stubborn resistance and lack of bombs.

Competing bombs: British Mills, German Stick and Egg Bombs. In the Bullecourt museum at the home of M. Letaille.

According to brigade orders, having reached O.G.2, the next stage required men of the 13th and 15th Battalions to go forward to capture Riencourt some 500 yards further on. Two German communication trenches, the Calwer Graben (Emu Alley) and the Cannstatter Graben (Ostrich Avenue) ran back from O.G.2 towards Riencourt. Captain D. Dunworth (15th Bn.) took a party of men, over the top, from O.G.2, with the intention of entering Ostrich Avenue from the side. The attackers came under fire from a machine gun, sited at the large six road junction. Most of the men were killed, but Dunworth, although wounded, managed to get into the part of Ostrich Avenue, adjacent to O.G.2, which had been evacuated by the enemy and

crawled back to O.G.2. A second party, led by Captain R.S. Somerville (16th Bn.), pushed forward in Emu Alley, until they reached the track running from the six road junction eastwards towards the Moulin Sans Souci. Here, in the increasing daylight, they were stopped by a machine gun firing from Riencourt.

In the meantime, more Australians were moving forward into the O.G. lines, but it soon became apparent that, with no tank support, huge losses in men and shortages of ammunition and bombs, further progress was impossible. Situation reports were sent back and orders given to secure the right flank, by blocking both trenches. Machine gun and Stokes mortar parties were brought forward. While this was being accomplished the enemy sent in two counter-attacks, from ground to the right, between O.G.1 and O.G.2. Vicious bomb fights ensued, the Germans using smaller egg-bombs and the Australians replying with Mills grenades. Both attacks were beaten off.

The 12th Brigade

The brigade was required to advance from 700 to 1,000 yards, with the Bullecourt salient on its left. It was hoped that protection would be afforded by the slope of the ground, and the bombardment, which was to be laid down on the village until 5.00 a.m. By this time, the Hindenburg Line should have been taken, rendering the tanks and the 46th Battalion free to enter the village. By 3.30 a.m. the 46th were in their jumping off trenches, but in the rush to issue the revised plans a mistake had been made in the orders sent to the commanding officer of the battalion, Lieutenant-Colonel H.K Dedham. Instead of being told to advance at zero hour, irrespective of the tanks, he was instructed to move forward fifteen minutes after the tanks had passed. The tanks allocated to the 12th Brigade were late, with the result that, as the 4th

Sunken section of Diagonal Road, from Bullecourt, just before it joined O.G. 2 at the Cross Memorial.

RIENCOURT CHURCH   SIX CROSS ROADS
DIAGONAL ROAD

Riencourt church, Diagonal Road and the Six Cross Roads from the direction of Bullecourt.

Brigade advanced, the two battalions of the 12th remained in their starting lines. By 5.10 a.m., with the dawn light getting stronger, and the barrage on Bullecourt lifted, the enemy observers directed fire at the 46th and 48th Battalions. Colonel Leane of the 48th, by now aware of the error, could not move until the 46th finally went forward, at 5. 15 a.m. Under intense fire, from the left flank, the 46th reached the wire, which was mostly unbroken. Some men, on the extreme right, went further to the right in search of breaks, but wandered into the central area, between the two brigades, where no attempt had been made to cut the wire. In the battalion centre, and on their left, O.G.1 was captured, the enemy fleeing back to O.G.2.

The 48th Battalion passed through the 46th and on to O.G.2, whereupon an immediate attempt was made to bomb eastwards, towards the 4th Brigade. This met with some success, but was stopped at Central Road. On its left, the battalion was lodged on the point where O.G.2 was crossed by a second road emanating from the six road junction. This sunken road, known as Diagonal Road, passed through O.G.2, continued, with O.G.2 on its right-hand side, before re-crossing it twice on its way to Bullecourt. By 7.00 a.m. the Australians held, about 500 yards of O.G.1, and about the same length of O.G.2, with an overlap in the middle, of about 250 yards. The two battalions were able to communicate through the cross trench "K".

Both brigades were now in serious trouble. They were short of ammunition and bombs and, having suffered heavy casualties, short of men. Under constant fire and repeated German counter-attacks, the battalion commanders requested that a protective barrage be laid along both flanks and along a line parallel with the Hindenburg Line, in front of Riencourt. The request was refused. Unknown to those at the front, the reports reaching the higher staff were indicating major successes.

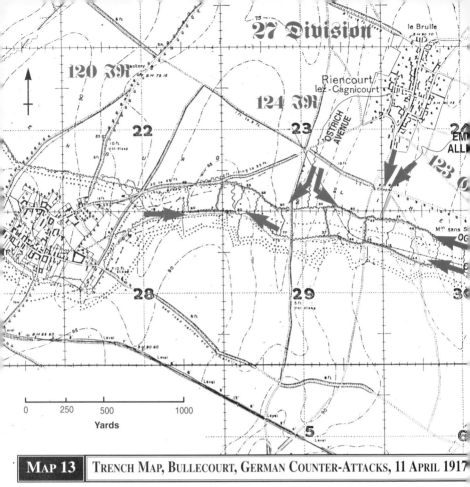

MAP 13 | **TRENCH MAP, BULLECOURT, GERMAN COUNTER-ATTACKS, 11 APRIL 1917**

Based on aerial and visual reports, they were informed that tanks and troops were in Riencourt and were moving on to Hendecourt. Bullecourt had also been occupied. How these reports came to be produced is far from clear, but given this information, any request for artillery support had to be refused. If a barrage had been permitted it would have fallen on friendly troops. So convinced was Gough of success, that he put the 4th Cavalry on the alert, and at 9.35 a.m. ordered them forward. They moved up towards the railway, but as the leaders crossed the Noreuil-Longatte road, they were caught by German artillery. Those further back were also shelled and at 10.30 a.m. the force was withdrawn.

By mid-morning it became clear to observers in the rear that what had at first been taken to be Australian troops in the vicinity of Riencourt were in fact German reinforcements moving up. At the same time, the failure of the tanks to reach beyond the Hindenburg Line was also admitted. At about 10.00 a.m., following a bombardment, the Germans counter-attacked from all directions **(See map 13)**. On the 4th Brigade front, vicious bomb fighting on the right, in both O.G.1 and O.G.2, drove the Australians back; they were also under attack in O.G.2 from Germans moving down Emu Alley. Eventually they had no alternative but to retire. So great were the numbers of wounded that many had to be left in dugouts in the two lines. By 11.45 a.m. the whole of the 4th Brigade's gains had been retaken. At the same time, on 12th Brigade front, the attack fell mainly on the 46th Battalion in O.G.1. Desperately tired and considerably under strength, they were driven out, also leaving many wounded behind. The 48th Battalion in O.G.2, unaware of the retirements until too late, tried to regain O.G.1 but without success. In the attempt, Captain Leane was wounded and died later in a German hospital. A full hour after the other battalions had retired what was left of the 48th struggled back to the railway, under an artillery barrage, which had finally been laid down on Bullecourt and Riencourt.

During the afternoon an unofficial cease-fire enabled many of the wounded lying out on the ground in front of the wire to make their way back to the railway. Other wounded, unable to struggle back, were brought in by medical orderlies. The Germans tended the wounded near their lines. However, this humane behaviour was not universal. Among the Australians taken prisoner was Captain D.P. Wells of the 13th Battalion, who had been severely wounded in the ground between O.G.1 and O.G.2. He was later repatriated from Germany, as an invalid, and parts of his official statement, produced on his return, are quoted in the 13th Battalion history.

> 'After capture no attempt was made to remove the wounded till dark, when German orderlies removed them, handling them very brutally without regard to the nature of their wounds. ...German Major put himself out to aggravate me and robbed me of all my belongings and badges of rank. ...Corporal Steward craved for a drink. He died soon after drinking. Then they handed the drink to me, when I found it to be paraffin, I would not drink. They were determined that I should drink it, and held me down and tried to force me. After that I was prepared for anything. They suddenly hastened out of the dug out pretending that the Australians were attacking again, in order to see what I would do. Knowing it to be a bluff, I remained still. I was roughly assisted out of the dug out. ...As far as I could see our men were lying everywhere and scores of Germans visiting and brutally

handling them, in their endeavour to rob them but no attempt was made to care for them or to have them removed. ...I have no hesitation in saying that hundreds must have died through exposure and sheer wilful neglect.' [10]

The Australians suffered over 3,000 casualties in the First Battle of Bullecourt. Most battalions lost about two thirds of their active strength. They lost more men taken prisoner, twenty-eight officers and in excess of 1,000 other ranks, than in any other action of the war. That Gough was at fault in the choice of the point of attack, a re-entrant, and in his reliance on the untried tanks, is indisputable. Nor can the decision to re-schedule the attack, twenty-four hours after the first failure be justified. The Australians were not to trust tanks again until the following year. Their trust in British generalship, already low after Fromelles and Pozières, was further lowered. The historian of the 14th Battalion summed up the results as follows:

'Officially, loss of the battle was attributed to the failure of the tanks, but real cause lay deeper. Extraordinary optimism of the Fifth Army staff in depending solely on an experiment with them, and the entirely inadequate conception of the staff of the magnitude of the task in hand. The whole seems to have been based on numerous misconceptions and was evidently the handwork of someone dominated, not by reason but by impulse.' [11]

The 62nd Division

At about 3 o'clock in the afternoon of 10 April, the Division received orders for the renewed attack on Bullecourt, scheduled for the following morning. The Australians were to clear the village as far west as the western exits. The 185th Brigade was then to advance one battalion, from the south-west, into Bullecourt and, supported by tanks, advance to capture the Hindenburg Line up to U.20.b.**(See map 14).** The 2/6 West Yorkshire (Lieutenant-Colonel J.H. Hastings) supported by the 2/8 West Yorkshire (Lieutenant-Colonel A.H. James), were detailed to occupy Bullecourt. By zero hour the 2/6 was in position, with two companies, A and D, on the railway at U.26.d and between C.2.b.7.9 and C.2.b.5.9 respectively. B Company was in support and C Company in reserve. Three hours later, the Division received a report that the Australians had taken Bullecourt. This did not agree with the observations of the West Yorkshires. No tanks had arrived and were certainly no Australians to be seen in the village. In spite of the confusion, patrols were ordered forward, to be followed by the battalion. The patrols reported that, on the south-western side of the village, the defences were intact and that snipers and machine guns were active, and that to attack would be suicidal. Accordingly, the battalion was recalled. Even so, two officers were killed and 61 other ranks listed as casualties.

The Division was subsequently criticised for not attacking but their actions were defended by Bean.

> *'But the widespread criticism of the 62nd Division for not coming to the 4th Division's assistance has no fair ground. It is true that the 62nd Division had shortly after 8 o'clock been ordered to send patrols to the Hindenburg Line, and that at 10.30 General Birdwood, realising the desperate plight of his troops, appealed to V Corps to attack. But the order at 8 o'clock was based on the definite assurance from I Anzac that no opposition had been met with in Bullecourt. The officers of the 62nd Division on the spot knew this to be untrue - except in the sense that no Australian soldier had been there. To have sent their unprotected infantry, without tanks, in broad daylight, over an approach as flat as a billiard table, against half-cut wire defended by a well warned enemy, in order to attempt a task which the 4th Australian Division had barely achieved by surprise in the breaking dawn would have been madness: three weeks later the commander of an Australian brigade refused to undertake practically the same operation in support of some of his own troops. The plight of the 4th Division, however desperate, would not have been in any degree alleviated by the useless sacrifice of British soldiers.'* [12]

First Bullecourt: The German perspective

Five days before the opening of the fighting at Bullecourt, the 27th (Württemberg) Division took over the line from Bullecourt to Quéant. The Division, part of XIV Reserve Corps (Quéant Group), commanded by Lieutenant-General Otto von Moser, was considered to be one of the best divisions in the German army. The positions of the three Regiments: 120th Infantry Regiment (I.R.), the 123rd Grenadier Regiment (G.R.) and the 124th Infantry Regiment were as shown **(See map 13)**. The 120th was to the west, in Bullecourt, the 124th across the line of the Australian attack and the 123rd, to the east, towards Quéant.

When the division moved into the still incomplete Hindenburg Line, it set about improving the defences and lines of communication,

| MAP 14 | TRENCH MAP, BULLECOURT, BRITISH 62ND DIVISION |

particularly between O.G.1 and O.G.2. They had insufficient time to do anything about the lack of trenches between Riencourt and O.G.2, which resulted in the majority of reinforcements having to come over open ground. Moser was well aware of the likelihood of an attack in support of the Arras offensive. In any attack he anticipated the involvement of tanks. To counter their effect, he ordered his artillery to set up special anti-tank guns, at this time, merely field guns firing over open sights. He also instructed all artillery units to concentrate on removing tanks from the battlefield.

According to several German regimental historians, the abortive

Australian attack on 10 April was not detected. The 120th I.R., from their position in Bullecourt, saw some movement but when itself attacked assumed that what had been observed was part of the same operation. As already noted, this attack was beaten back with heavy losses to the 62nd Division. During the remainder of the day, troop movements were detected by the Germans and, given the reports from the 120th I.R. and artillery activity, it was not surprising that they were prepared for an attack the following morning. In the centre, the 124th I.R. first detected the sound of engines at about 2.00 a.m., and at 4.30 a.m. saw the Australians approaching and working on the barbed wire. Fifteen minutes later, the noise of the engines intensified and several tanks were seen approaching. The subsequent fighting is recorded in the divisional history.

'Our defenders came up on the parapet and were shooting and throwing hand grenades into the attacking masses. Our machine guns mowed down the English* in rows but again and again the successive waves came on and came closer to our trenches. Every man had fired off 70 rounds and then close combat started. The first company on the right was overwhelmed, 20 men, and the team serving a heavy machine gun were shot down. The company commander, Leutnant Mohr, immediately brought up a reserve platoon, for a counter-attack, but leading this, he was soon killed by a hand grenade. This attack had initially some success and pushed back the English but soon we ran out of hand grenades. The enemy used this opportunity, and repelled the attack.'

What was left of the first company fell back to the sunken road

* Moser refers to the English incorrectly. The 124th was attacked by the Australians.

Stretcher bearers bringing out wounded in O.G.1 IWM E(Aus) 440

behind O.G.2, Diagonal Road, leaving the defence in the hands of the companies on their left. In spite of the presence of tanks these managed to stem the advance, although the tenth and eleventh companies in the centre, eventually fell back after suffering heavy losses. On the extreme left the twelfth, and parts of the eleventh company, held their ground against all attacks. In this successful defence they were assisted by units of the 123rd Grenadiers. By 8.30 in the morning the British had captured part of the Calwer Graben, together with parts of the first and second lines. The ninth company of the 124th, which had moved forward during the night, drove the enemy out of the Calwer Graben, but then, due to a false report, withdrew, thinking itself surrounded. The situation was becoming critical, so decisive action was needed. The local commander ordered counter-attacks to be launched: the ninth and fifth companies, through the Calwer Graben, the seventh company on their left and the sixth and eight companies on their right.' [13]

This was to be the counter-attack launched on the Australians at about 10 o'clock.

'The ninth company of the 124th and Leutnant Slotterbeck, quickly made their way in through the Calwer Graben and attacked the enemy in the second line, and occupied this, as far as the right wing of the Grenadiers. ...When the seventh company of the 124th advanced towards the mill, the enemy who had

Wounded German prisoners and Australian Red Cross wagons in Noreuil Valley. IWM E(Aus) 446

View down the Noreuil Valley.

advanced as far as this, was surrounded on all sides, because the sixth and eight companies, of the 124th had, by this time ,on the right wing, retaken the second line, and the communication trenches. While the surrounded English were being taken back to Riencourt, the assaulting troops, encouraged by the success, stormed across open country and took back the first line of trenches. ...At 3 o'clock in the afternoon this sector was once again completely in the hands of the regiment. Hundreds of English dead lay on the front, especially where breakthroughs had been made in front of machine guns, on the road between Riencourt and Noreuil.' [14]

Losses in the regiment were heavy: six officers killed and five wounded, among other ranks, there were 144 dead, 230 wounded and 62 missing.

On the front held by the 123rd Grenadier Regiment, it was 3 a.m. when the first sound of engines was reported. Moser gives a graphic account of the approach and capture of a tank by this regiment. The tank, No. 799, Lieutenant Davies, was the one which veered to the extreme right and entered the Balkon-Stellung.

'At a speed of about four kilometres an hour, the tank approached the barbed wire, firing. After a short stop, he drove along the wire, easily crossed the wire, on the left sector of our front and then, from the flank, fired on our front line. For the first time the grenadiers were facing one of these notorious monsters. ...Our infantry moved aside, and

67

let the tank cross over the first trench, and in doing so, he was firing to all sides. As it grew light, he became the target of heavy fire from our infantry, from our mortars and from our artillery. Above all, it was due to Leutnant Scharbel, the leader of our Third Machine Gun Company, who was able to organise the resistance, and who brought a machine gun, some one hundred metres forward, put it into position and working single handed, brought it to bear on the tank. From a distance of about one hundred and fifty metres, he fired off twelve hundred rounds of ammunition at it. The tank tried to turn its more lightly armoured side away from this hail of bullets, but too late. Clouds of smoke arose, from the tank, flames as well, and they revealed that he had been mortally struck at something like fifty metres behind the first line of trenches. The men in the tank suffered both gunshot wounds and injuries from burning, they tried to escape, but were taken. ...The tank shot up by Leutnant Scharbel was the first which had been put out of action inside German lines, and for days, officers of all ranks, some coming from a great distance, came to look at this strange beast.'[15]

When the 124th counter-attacked, through the centre it was aided by units from the two flanking regiments. It was this combined assault, on three sides, which led to the withdrawal of the Australians and the capture of so many of their number. The German losses, small in comparison with those of the British side, were 749 including 42 prisoners. The 27th Division considered the day to be one of the most glorious in their annals.

Bibliography

1 *The Official History of Australia in the War 1914-1918.* Volume IV. Bean. 1933.
2 *A Company of Tanks.* Major W.H.L. Watson. 1917.
3 *Military Operations in France & Belgium. 1917* Volume I. Falls. Macmillan 1940.
4 Ibid.
5 *The Official History of Australia in the War 1914-1918.* Volume IV. Bean. 1933.
6 *Military Operations in France & Belgium. 1917* Volume I. Falls. Macmillan 1940.
7 *War Diary 1st Tank Corps* HQ. Public Record Office. WO 95/97
8 *A Company of Tanks.* Major W.H.L. Watson. 1917.
9 *The Official History of Australia in the War 1914-1918.* Volume IV. Bean. 1933.
10 *The History of the Thirteenth Battalion AIF.* Thomas A. White. Sydney 1924.
11 *The History of the Fourteenth Battalion AIF.* Newton Wanliss. Melbourne. 1929
12 *The Official History of Australia in the War 1914-1918.* Volume IV. Bean. 1933.
13 *Die Württemberger im Weltkrieg.* Otto von Moser.
14 Ibid.
15 Ibid.

Chapter Three

THE GERMAN ASSAULT AT LAGNICOURT

When the Australian 4th Division attacked on 11 April, it did so on a front of 2,750 yards. To its left, the British 62nd Division held about 4,000 yards, but to its right, the Australian 1st Division, held the line for 12,000 yards from a point south of Riencourt to the Canal du Nord, near Havrincourt. The 1st Division was responsible for almost two thirds of the entire Fifth Army front. That one division could hold such a huge stretch followed from the fact that, the German withdrawal, in that sector, was only just complete. In fact, they still held a number of outpost positions in front of their defence lines. The Australian division was disposed 'in depth' which involved four lines of defence **(See map 15)**:

a Corps Reserve Line, about 5 - 6 miles back, not shown on map 15
a Corps Main Line, 3 - 5 miles back
a Second Line, in front of the line of villages, Morchies - Beaumetz
a Forward Line of Resistance.

The Forward Line consisted of several lines: a reserve line, a support line and a front line. The last, made up of small outpost trenches, or picquet lines, in front of the villages, Lagnicourt - Boursies - Demicourt - Hermies, was behind a line of sentry groups.

On 13 April, the Australian 4th Division was relieved by the Australian 2nd Division, with the 5th and 6th Brigades in the line. The 5th Brigade, on

The Daily Telegraph,
Monday 7 May 1917.

FIGHT FOR LAGNICOURT.

HEAVY GERMAN LOSSES.

BRITISH HEADQUARTERS (FRANCE),
Monday.

The attack which the Germans launched against our positions between Hermies and Noreuil at dawn yesterday morning was very interesting from the tactical point of view, first of all as one of the best examples we have yet had of what may be termed old-fashioned field warfare, and secondly as demonstrating the great superiority of our troops in this species of fighting. Indeed, it is becoming increasingly clear that the Germans, regarding their lines as impregnable, and, therefore, concluding that defensive strategy would require no more than that they should hold them until the end of the war, have been training their new troops almost wholly in trench warfare. Our method, on the other hand, has been to rehearse our men for the open fighting, which we have been praying for now for two and three-quarter years, and which has come at last. The German papers have been boasting about what their wonderful field-greys would do when they met our men in the open. The German soldiers have so far only succeeded in making their papers once more look ridiculous. Fritz is no match for Tommy in a hand-to-hand fight, and it does not improve his moral that he is beginning clearly to realise this, as yesterday's fighting proved.

The one spot where a very temporary success was attained was upon a rather important spur north of the village of Boursies. Here the Germans pressed on with great determination, and our posts were driven in by the overwhelming weight of numbers. The enemy also got into the edge of the Lagnicourt ruins, and appeared satisfied with his success, as he made no attempt to push on. His victory was very short-lived, however. At 7.30 our men, who had fallen back having rested, were reformed and stiffened by supports, and, under cover of a barrage like a dust-storm, went forward to counter-attack. They advanced by alternate companies, one halting and firing while the other moved on under this flanking fusillade, these tactics being carried on along the whole front of the attack. As a spectacle it was reminiscent of a field-day on manœuvres. As practical warfare in the open it was so brilliantly successful that by the time the positions had been entirely recarried, after three hours of occupation by the enemy, 1,500 German corpses lay among the very much larger number of wounded, and 300 prisoners were in our hands. By a most conservative computation this attack cannot have cost the Huns less than two-thirds of a division in casualties. Within a few hours after it had been launched these losses were all the enemy had to show for their effort.—*Reuter's Special Service.*

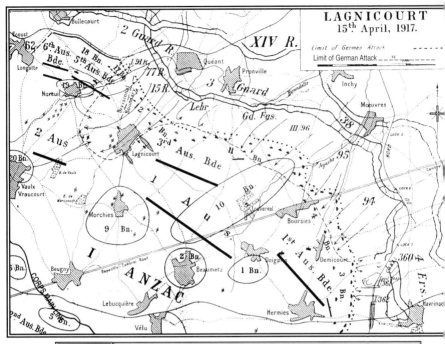

MAP 15 | LAGNICOURT, GERMAN ATTACK 15 APRIL 1917

the right, had two battalions, the 17th and 18th in the line, and one each in support and reserve. The support battalion, the 19th, was near Noreuil and the reserve, the 20th, at Vaulx Vraucourt. On the same night the 1st Division pushed its posts forward to within one thousand yards of the Hindenburg Line. General Gough, already planning for a renewed attack on Bullecourt, using the 2nd Division, considered that by moving the 1st Division forward he might mislead the enemy into thinking that a renewed attack would be in their area. As a result of the move, the new line was fan-shaped and covered an additional one thousand yards. The 1st Brigade, held the front between the Bapaume-Cambrai road and the Canal du Nord. The brigade had two battalions, the 3rd and the 4th in the line. The 1st and 2nd Battalions were in reserve at Doignies and Beaumetz respectively. From Louverval to the divisional boundary, between Noreuil and Lagnicourt, the line was held by the 11th and 12th Battalions of the 3rd Brigade. The reserve battalions, the 9th and 10th, were at Morchies and Louverval, but four companies, two from each of the reserves, were in closer support to the battalions in the line. The 2nd Brigade was in reserve, on the Corps Main Line. As part of the preparations for the 2nd Division attack artillery, required to cut the belts of wire in front of the Hindenburg Line, had been brought forward into the Lagnicourt, Noreuil and Ecoust valleys.

General von Moser was anxious to harass the British at every opportunity. On 13 April he was informed that, in readiness for any attack on his front, XIV Reserve Corps was to be reinforced by the addition of the 3rd Guard Division. His response was to propose that he pre-empt any such action by attacking while the Australians were still recovering from their efforts on the 11 April. Such an attack would have a dual purpose: it would thwart an attack by the enemy and might also draw British reserves away from Arras. His proposal was accepted by army headquarters, who were so taken with the plan that two further divisions, those adjoining his left flank, were added to his Corps for the operation, code named 'Sturmbok'.

At 4.00 a.m. on 15 April, the 1st Division and the 17th Battalion, on the right of the 2nd Division, were attacked, by units of four German divisions, part of General Moser's XIV Reserve Corps. South of the Bapaume-Cambrai road the 4th Ersatz Division fell upon the 3rd and 4th Battalions. The 3rd managed to repel the attack but, due in part to the undulating terrain, the 4th Battalion was eventually forced to fall back to a line passing close to Demicourt, and through the outskirts of Boursies.

Further north, on the far side of the Bapaume-Cambrai road, the attack on the 3rd Brigade, by the 38th Division, was prefaced by a brief but intense bombardment. Two picquets, on the left flank, managed to hold up the 38th but on the right, in front of Louverval, the enemy, by infiltrating along a gully, managed to get between and behind the Australians. The flank picquet gradually withdrew until it reached a sunken road where it held on. The Germans came under machine gun fire from the supports, under Captain R. Hemingway. Many were killed but some managed to enter an old trench, which effectively surrounded the picquet. Lieutenant C. Pope, the officer in charge, sent a runner, Private Gledhill, for ammunition, which was despatched along with fifteen reinforcements. Unfortunately, in the growing light of day, it proved impossible to reach Pope. Other posts were also surrounded. Pope was eventually shot through the head and killed, and the posts overrun. However, by their dogged resistance time was gained and a new line formed in the rear by the reserve companies and

Site of Captain Sheppard's action across the Noreuil valley.

CAPTAIN SHEPPARDS' POSITION   NOREUIL VALLEY

NOREUIL

QUÉANT

German Machine Gun Position

two companies of the 12th Battalion. For his gallantry Pope was posthumously awarded the Victoria Cross.

Further north still, the right of the 12th Battalion was not attacked until after the main assault. It held its line but, in daylight, hordes of Germans were observed behind its line, in Lagnicourt. It immediately fell back to reserve positions to face the enemy. The left flank, along with the right flank of the 2nd Division, the 17th Battalion, was attacked by the 2nd Guards Reserve Division. Both units blamed each other for what occurred, but in truth it is likely that neither was at fault. They were attacked, without warning, in such overwhelming strength, that the probability is that they fell back simultaneously. In the sunken road between Lagnicourt and Noreuil **(See map 16)** Captain A.S. Vowles, 12th Battalion, was alerted to the approach of the enemy up the spur between Lagnicourt and Noreuil, across which the sunken road ran.

> 'His Lewis gunners drove them back to shelter, but almost immediately others were discovered approaching from Lagnicourt to the right rear, and a machine gun opened from that direction. On Vowles' left front, in another road slightly in advance of that which he occupied, was a section (four guns) of the 21st Machine Gun Company. ...One gun lay packed ready for moving; the others had hardly had time to open when some of the enemy from Lagnicourt appeared close in their rear. There was a short bomb fight. A gunner Private Erbacher, by swinging his gun round and firing into the Germans only fifteen yards in rear, drove them back, dismantled his gun, and, with a few others, managed to get through them; but in a tight corner the gun had to be left hidden in a shell-hole, and was not recovered. The Germans, after overwhelming these machine gunners, passed on and attacked Vowles, and at the same time others appeared from the direction of Lagnicourt, cutting him off from his battalion headquarters. ...At about 4.30, to avoid being surrounded and destroyed, he gave the word to withdraw up the valley towards Vaulx-Vraucourt, where were some reserves of the 2nd Division.'[1]

As already noted, artillery, had been brought forward in preparation for the new attack on Bullecourt. The 2nd Brigade, the foremost of the 1st

Australian 1st Brigade artillery positions 15 April 1917.

AUSTRALIAN 1ST BRIGADE ARTILLERY POSITIONS 15 APRIL 1917

LAGNICOURT

D 36

VAULX-VRAUCOURT

CAPTAIN VOWLES   LAGNICOURT CHURCH

Site of Captain Vowles' action 15 April 1917.

Division's artillery, was located in Lagnicourt, not far from Vowles' position, and the 1st Brigade, along with the group headquarters, nearby. The batteries could not open fire, for fear of hitting their own troops, but at 5.00 a.m., when the guns were under rifle fire, the 2nd Brigade were ordered to open fire if the enemy was visible. At the same time, they were ordered to prepare to abandon the guns, but to remove their breech blocks and dial sights. Shortly afterwards, hand-grenades started to fall around the guns, so all four batteries of the 2nd Brigade, were abandoned. On the other side of Lagnicourt, the picquets of the 17th Battalion were also forced back, into a sunken road in front of Noreuil **(See map 17)**. Here Captain W.H. Sheppard, with Lieutenant C.H. Dakin, attempted to hold the line with machine guns, but the enemy, on the other side of the valley, succeeded in establishing a machine gun to enfilade Sheppard's position, so Sheppard decided to fall back on the trench close behind it.

> 'The left of Sheppard's company duly withdrew to it, but the right was under too heavy fire. A few men, attempting to cross the open, were killed...the enemy penetrated along the bottom of the valley, lined the bank there in rear of the road, and set up a machine gun close in front of Noreuil. Lieutenant Dakin, commanding the 5th Company's four machine guns, was shot by the enemy from this direction, and the Australians remaining in the road, about thirty in number, were initially charged from the right and captured. The enemy lined the road and placed two machine guns there. All the subalterns of Sheppard's company had been wounded. ...But the enemy's advance was stayed.'[2]

As the Germans swept forward, men of the 12th Battalion were forced

The lane, slightly in advance of Captain Vowles's position, where the section of the Australian 21st Machine Gun Company was sited.

to give ground, and to the east of Lagnicourt Captain J. Newland led his men back half-way to the support lines, before ordering them to take refuge in the sunken road between Lagnicourt and Doignies, at about 5.00 a.m. By this time, such had been the speed of the German advance, that the battalion headquarters, south-east of the Noreuil, was threatened. The battalion commander, Lieutenant-Colonel C.H. Elliot, rounded up all cooks, batmen and others at the headquarters, and set up a line along the edge of the sunken road, to hold off the enemy coming down the valley to the west of Lagnicourt. Here they were eventually joined by a company of the 9th Battalion from Morchies. The thrust was finally stopped at about 6.30 a.m., but not before the guns of the 1st Brigade had also been lost.

Meanwhile, the Germans were attempting to move forward around the eastern side of the village. Here they came under fire from Newland's group in the Lagnicourt-Doignies road. They, in turn, now found themselves under fire from the enemy coming through Lagnicourt. Firing from both banks of the road the movement was held, but when the Germans set up a machine gun on the edge of the village to fire down the road they were in serious danger. The situation was relieved by Sergeant J.W. Whittle, who ran out, on his own, to attack the gun crew before they could open fire. To reach them, he had to cross open ground under continuous fire. He killed the crew and returned with the gun. The position was then held until reinforcements arrived. For their actions that day, and during the earlier attack on Boursies, both Newland and Whittle were awarded the Victoria Cross.

By now the situation was becoming clearer. So much so, that a barrage was put down between Lagnicourt and Noreuil, which, in conjunction with the efforts of the infantry, prevented the enemy moving forward from Lagnicourt. The scene was now set for an Australian counter-attack. Following the break-through, Brigadier-General R. Smith, commanding the 5th Brigade, set about rectifying the situation. He ordered the 19th Battalion, at Noreuil, to form a flank for the defence of the village, on the ridge between it and Lagnicourt and the 20th to move to the high ground near the Bois de Vaulx. South of Lagnicourt, Lieutenant-Colonel Elliot was reinforced by two more companies of the 9th Battalion. The two forces met at about 7 a.m.

The sunken road, between Lagnicourt and Doignies, where Captain Newland and Sergeant Whittle carried out the second of the actions for which they were each awarded the Victoria Cross.

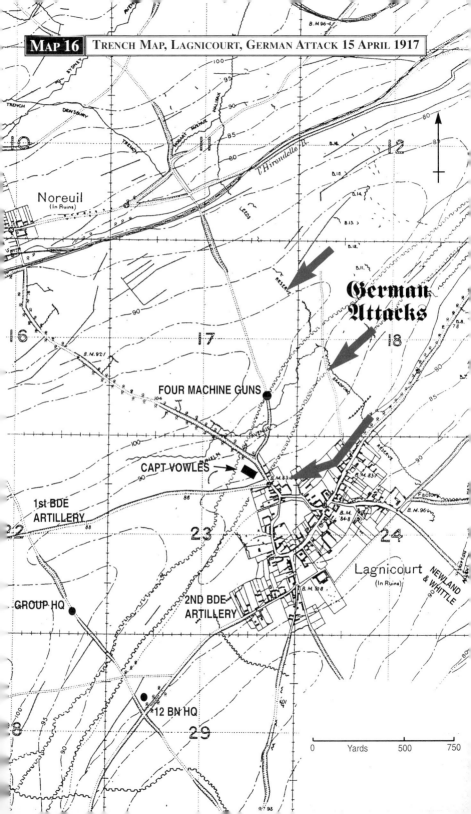

MAP 16 | TRENCH MAP, LAGNICOURT, GERMAN ATTACK 15 APRIL 1917

Noreuil
(In Ruins)

German Attacks

FOUR MACHINE GUNS

CAPT VOWLES

1st BDE ARTILLERY

2ND BDE ARTILLERY

GROUP HQ

12 BN HQ

Lagnicourt
(In Ruins)

NEWLAND & WHITTLE

Factory

0   Yards   500   750

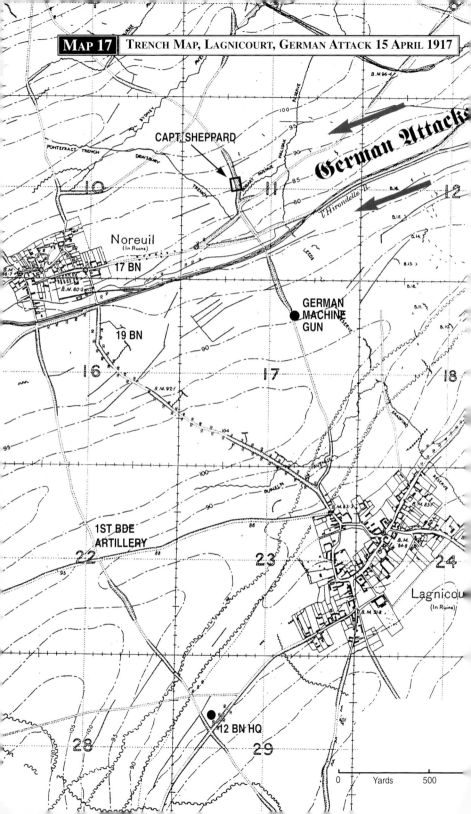

MAP 17 **TRENCH MAP, LAGNICOURT, GERMAN ATTACK 15 APRIL 1917**

CAPT SHEPPARD

German Attacks

l'Hirondelle R.

Noreuil
(In Ruins)

17 BN

GERMAN
MACHINE
GUN

19 BN

1ST BDE
ARTILLERY

Lagnicou
(In Ruins)

12 BN HQ

0   Yards   500

'Since daylight the Germans in their self-created salient had been shot at from all sides. They were already dispirited, with little stomach left for a fight. At the first sign of a counter-attack they collapsed.

The counter-attack was begun, it would seem, by the companies of the 9th Battalion, on Lieutenant-Colonel Elliot's initiative, and taken up first by the 20th Battalion and soon afterwards - as soon as they could get the barrage lifted - by the 19th from the direction of Noreuil. Observing that their opponents were flinching, eager to pay off their heavy score, the Australians on the flanks of both divisions pressed forward. Many Germans surrendered; many others were shot down; in the rear, formed bodies, were heading back for the Hindenburg Line. The heavy artillery, apprised of this fact by a report from the air, laid every available gun on the wire to catch the enemy as he retreated through the sally-ports. There was a slight delay in clearing the northern end of Lagnicourt, on which the British barrage still lay, but once that lifted the forward flow of the Australians was resumed, and the position was soon completely restored.' [3]

By mid-afternoon, the enemy was again being pounded by the very guns that he had had in his possession for some two hours. When those of the 1st Brigade were recovered, they were all found to be undamaged, as were all but five of those belonging to the 2nd Brigade. However, the Germans believed that twenty-two guns had been destroyed.

In the course of the fighting the Australians suffered 1,010 casualties, of which only four were officers. The 17th and 11th Battalions were the most affected, suffering 181 and 245 casualties respectively. In addition, there were 357 men listed as missing, of whom 80 per cent were subsequently identified as prisoners.

On the German side, the total losses were given as 2,313, with very little to show for this expenditure of men and materials. Only at one point had the objective been reached. There were no movements of troops from the Arras front and no delays were caused in the preparations for the renewed attack at Bullecourt. In the event, the battalions which suffered most on 15 April, were fit enough to play a full part in the forthcoming battle.

Bibliography

1 *The Official History of Australia in the War 1914-1918.* Volume IV. Bean. 1933.
2 Ibid.
3 *Military Operations in France & Belgium. 1917* Volume 1. Falls. Macmillan 1940

Chapter Four

SECOND BATTLE OF BULLECOURT

Throughout the month of April, the Battle of Arras continued. The British gains were minimal but the casualty figures were high, e.g. on 23rd, actions around Guémappe resulted in some 16,000 losses. On the 28th, seven divisions of the First and Third Armies advanced on a front of eight miles but, following the German counter-attack, part of their strategy of 'Defence in Depth', the only gain was a small area to the east of Monchy-le-Preux. The Fifth Army was not involved in these actions, but was given a role in the offensive scheduled for 3 May. This attack was to be on a grand scale: a front of sixteen miles, involving a total of fourteen divisions. On the extreme right the Fifth Army would make another attempt to break into the Hindenburg Line at Bullecourt. Vital lessons had been learned from the failure of the previous month. No longer would the Australians attack unaided. Although still required to assault the re-entrant east of the village, with a final

Aerial view of the eastern side of Bullecourt, see map 9. Tank Museum

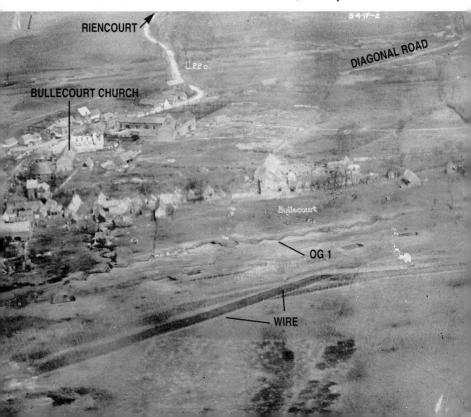

Australian 18-pounder in the Noreuil Valley May 1917. IWM E(Aus),601

objective beyond Riencourt, the Australians would be supported by a simultaneous attack by the British 62nd Division. A preliminary artillery bombardment would also be included. During April, I Anzac Corps was allocated an extra twelve batteries of heavy artillery, bringing it up to a total strength of 31 batteries. V Corps was similarly strengthened. By the middle of the month, the last building in Bullecourt had been demolished and both Riencourt and Hendecourt were in ruins. The gun positions were in exposed valleys and sunken roads. Bean describes the conditions under which the crews laboured:

> *'Noreuil Valley, which the Germans knew to be lined with guns, was constantly drenched with gas-shells. The gas officer of the Corps, Lieutenant H.W. Wilson, reported that on the night of April 20 the Germans fired into it 3,000 lethal shells, the bombardment lasting for five hours. On the night of the 21st they shelled it for four hours with 1,000 lethal shells, and on the following night for an hour with 700 lethal and lachrymatory shells.'* [1]

Gough had hoped to renew his offensive in April but as the month progressed and no new attack was ordered, he used the time to prepare the Anzacs as never before. The Australian 2nd Division, scheduled to carry out the attack on Bullecourt, planned and rehearsed every detail of the attack. The scheme detailed three objectives: the two trenches O.G.1 and O.G.2, and the capture of Bullecourt village by the 62nd Division; the Fontaine-Moulin Sans Souci road, as a starting point for the third phase, and an advance on Riencourt (2nd Division) and Hendecourt (62nd Division).

The final line of the advance was shaped like half an ellipse. It ran to the west of Bullecourt, then north-east to pass behind Hendecourt, where it turned south to pass behind Riencourt and on towards Lagnicourt. Tanks would again feature, but this time, they would assist the 62nd Division. After their experiences in April, the Australians preferred to attack without tanks.

The Australian staff, aware of the consequences on 11 April of the failure to get ammunition to the troops in OG Lines, ensured that the infantry and other specialist units went forward with supplies sufficient for holding the first objective. In addition, massive supply dumps were established for each brigade on the line of the railway. In turn, these were supplied from two larger dumps at Igri Corner just north of Noreuil. Finally, the artillery bombardment was augmented with large numbers of gas shells, and the belts of wire blown apart by means of Bangalore torpedoes, long metal tubes filled with ammonal.

Sketch of a Bangalore Torpedo. PRO WO 95/3068

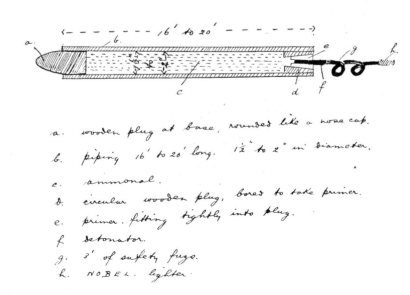

Rough Sketch of Bangalore Torpedo.

a. wooden plug at base, rounded like a nose cap.
b. piping 16' to 20' long. 1½" to 2" in diameter.
c. ammonal.
d. circular wooden plug, bored to take primer.
e. primer. fitting tightly into plug.
f. detonator.
g. 3' of safety fuse.
h. NOBEL. lighter.

The Australian 2nd Division

The plan required that the division employ two brigades, the 5th (Brigadier-General R. Smith) and the 6th (Brigadier-General J. Gellibrand), to the right and left of Central Road respectively **(See Map 18)**. There was to be no gap between them, unlike the situation on 11 April, and each brigade was to commit four battalions. The artillery would keep up a steady barrage until the assault commenced, at which time a heavy barrage would be laid on the enemy front and support lines, with a lighter one on No Man's Land. A creeping barrage, advancing initially at a rate of 100 yards every three minutes, would protect the infantry. Once the infantry reached the Hindenburg Line, bombers would move out, east and west, to extend the line.

Zero hour was 3.45 a.m., by which time both brigades were in position. On the right the 17th and 19th Battalions, with the 18th and 20th Battalions in support, were in front of the sunken road running from Bullecourt to Quéant. On the left the 22nd and 24th Battalions were in front of the sunken road, supported by the 21st Battalion, in and near the road, and the 23rd Battalion between the road and the line of the railway.

The 5th Brigade

According to the precisely-timed schedule, both O.G.1 and O.G.2 should have been taken by 4.20 a.m. Observers reported seeing the success flares from both brigades. When the leading waves of the 5th Brigade reached the wire, they were held up by intense machine gun fire, both from the German lines ahead and from enfilade positions. Succeeding waves coming through were also caught and, in the ensuing panic, an order to retire was given. The rear waves, unaware of what was happening, saw men coming back and followed suit. By 4.45 a.m. about 400 unwounded men were back in the sunken road leaving many others trapped in shell holes near the German line. Gellibrand at his headquarters on the railway realised that, if the failure of the 5th Brigade was not rectified, the whole operation could falter. He ordered two of his staff officers, Captain W.J. Gilchrist and Lieutenant D.N. Rentoul, to rally the returned troops and with a company of the 26th Battalion (7th Brigade) under Major P.J. Thorn, to return to the Hindenburg Line. On the way, they were joined by Lieutenant-Colonel G.F. Murphy of the 18th Battalion. Bean gives a graphic account of what followed:

'No artillery barrage covered them. They advanced at a

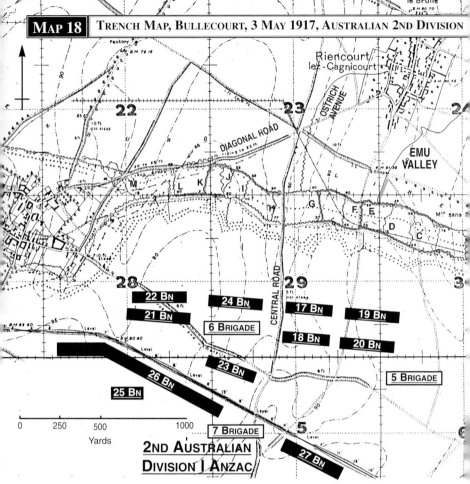

steady walk, rifles slung or at the trail, through the German artillery barrage and under fire of a few snipers until near the entanglement, when German machine guns opened. The stream of bullets from two guns could be seen ripping up the ground and raising two small dust-clouds which gradually converged until they met. The troops were passing shell-holes crowded with their mates, who had been sheltering there since the first attack, and they began to take cover. Of the leaders, who were systematically picked off by German snipers, many of the finest were again hit. Rentoul had been wounded before reaching the wire, and was later killed. Of the 26th, Major Thorne and Lieutenants Major, Homer and Lanyon were hit - the last two mortally, both splendid officers. The 18th Battalion in its double attempt lost, killed or wounded, 12 of its 22 officers engaged, and 61 of its 84 N.C.Os.

Second Lieutenant H.W. Homer
Brookwood Cemetery Surrey

Colonel Murphy moved across to steady first the right and then the left, but the advance ended slightly beyond the wire. Only on the left did three men led by Captain Gilchrist - and still further to that flank, under the cover of the Central Road, two parties under Lieutenants Davies and Irvine of the 18th Battalion - enter O.G.1.' [2]

Lieutenant H.W. Homer MM was born in Kington, Herefordshire in 1894. He subsequently died in hospital in England and is buried in the Australian plot at Brookwood Military Cemetery, Surrey.

In O.G.1 Gilchrist ran into Lieutenant E. Smythe of the 24th Battalion, who gave him a situation report. Gilchrist went on down the trench where he collected the men of the 6th Brigade and attempted to bomb his way eastwards, but was almost immediately driven back. At almost the same instant, the 6th Brigade was driven back in O.G.2 leaving the Hindenburg Line east of Central Road in German hands. It was now 6.00 a.m. Not to be denied, Gilchrist reorganised his mixed party of men and, when joined by about 30 men of the 5th Brigade, returned to the attack. The Germans were driven back to the cross-trench "G", in the course of which advance a machine gun was captured and turned on the enemy in Riencourt. At about 7.00 a.m. the tables were turned and the Germans regained all the lost ground, forcing the small band back to Central Road. During the Australian advance Gilchrist was seen jumping on to the parapet to throw bombs but when the counter-attack was held he had vanished, and was never seen again.

The 6th Brigade

The 24th Battalion, closely followed by the 23rd, advanced over ground which lay in a depression and was, therefore, sheltered from the worst of the enemy fire. Those on the extreme right were also able to seek cover under the sunken, eastern side of Central Road. When they reached the wire, the barrage had just moved forward, and they entered O.G.1 before the enemy had time to reorganise. Seeing no members of the 5th Brigade, Lieutenant Smythe led a party of the 24th Battalion about 200 yards to the right before he was stopped by a party of Germans manning a machine gun. The following waves of the two battalions passed over O.G.1, kept close to the creeping barrage and succeeded in taking a stretch of O.G.2 with little resistance. Again, it was clear that no support lay to the right, so Lieutenant R. Pickett followed the example set by Lieutenant Smythe and led a party off in that direction. He occupied O.G.2 as far as cross-trench "G", at the same time blocking off the passage of reinforcements down Ostrich Avenue.

On the left flank, the 22nd and 21st Battalions did not fare so well. Like the left flank on 11 April, they suffered heavily under enfilade fire from the German defences in Bullecourt. The line of advance was also split by heavy artillery fire. The attackers were forced to move either side of this fire. Those on the right managed to enter O.G.1 and press on to O.G.2, but on the left, the delay gave the enemy time to reorganise and the majority were pinned down in shell-holes some way short of O.G.1. Only very few reached O.G.1 and moved on to O.G.2 where they were later joined by some men from the later waves. They reached O.G.2 via the cross-trench "I". There now followed a serious of vicious bomb fights in both O.G. lines as the Australians tried to move westwards to reach the prescribed line of the left flank. Those in O.G.2 came up against the same problem as the 48th Battalion on 11 April, namely the junction of O.G.2 with Diagonal Road. Here the fighting was led by Lieutenant J.E. Jennings, 21st Battalion, who had all the fingers of his left hand blown off but continued to fight, only to be killed shortly after. At about 6.00 a.m. a party of Germans was observed moving towards the Australians in the ground between O.G.1 and O.G.2. A bombing party moved down cross-trench "K" and, supported by rifle and machine gun fire, quickly drove the enemy back.

While the fighting in O.G.1 and O.G.2 continued, the time-table required that the troops designated to capture the remaining objectives move out into the ground beyond O.G.2. Led by Captain G.L. Maxfield, the fourth wave of the 24th Battalion managed to reach the second objective of their battalion. This included the line of a trench tramway which ran from the point where six roads converged, the Six Cross Roads, north-westwards before turning to run parallel with the trench system and then back into Bullecourt **(See map 19)**. The troops detailed to capture the third objective, four waves of the 23rd Battalion, led by Captain J. Pascoe, moved to the right and used the protection afforded by Central Road to reach a point close to the Six Cross Roads. It was now sufficiently light for Pascoe to observe that the 5th Brigade had not passed O.G.2, indeed he could see Germans standing on the

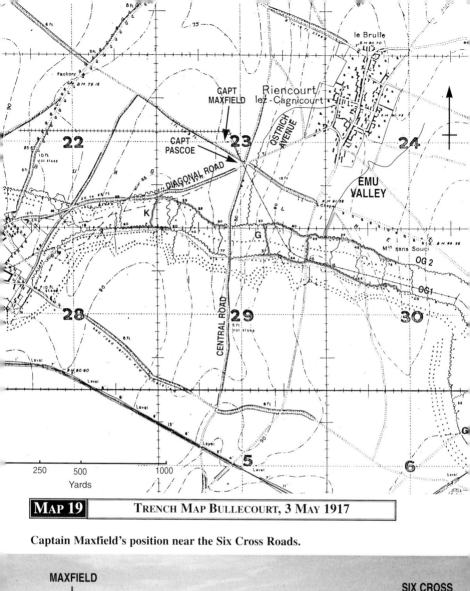

Map 19   Trench Map Bullecourt, 3 May 1917

Captain Maxfield's position near the Six Cross Roads.

parapet in Emu Alley, firing into the Australians. With the failure on the 6th Brigade's left, the position of the men looking to capture the second and third objectives was precarious. An attempt was made to send reinforcements to Maxfield but the Germans set up a machine gun to his left firing along the line of the tramway which made any movement impossible. With Maxfield were two other officers, Lieutenant J. Harris and Lieutenant H.L. Rhynehart, and about 30 men. Gradually the numbers increased until he had almost 100 including another officer, Lieutenant R.D. Desmond of the 6th Australian Machine Gun Company, with two Vickers machine guns. These machine guns, together with a Lewis gun, were able to pour fire in the direction of Riencourt. However, the Germans could be seen assembling in Ostrich Avenue ready to launch a counter-attack. Meantime, communication had been established with Maxfield, who asked for artillery to take out two machine guns in the Artillerie Schutzstellung which were hampering all movement near the tramway. The expected counter-attack was launched at 8.50 a.m., down Ostrich Avenue, but was beaten back at the barricade near the Six Cross Roads. At the same time, the Germans laid down a fierce barrage on the ground between the Hindenburg Line and the railway embankment. Under cover of this barrage they attempted to bomb along the O.G.1 and O.G.2 but were beaten back at all points. The first major counter-attack was held but the losses sustained by the Australians meant that reinforcements were urgently needed, particularly by the 5th Brigade east of the Central Road. The remaining battalion of the 7th Brigade, the 28th, was ordered forward. By mid-morning Gellibrand knew that the line held by Maxfield could not be sustained and he ordered the position to be abandoned. Maxfield had already lost the services of Lieutenants Harris and Rhynehart to enemy fire and, shortly after, Lieutenant Desmond was killed by artillery fire from the Australian lines. Maxfield started back but was never seen again. At noon, Gellibrand was able to re-position the line of the Australian barrage to protect the men remaining in the Hindenburg Line.

At mid-day observers reported that large numbers of Germans were moving, in the open, in front of Riencourt. Shortly after the German artillery increased its rate of fire: on the railway embankment and on the land between the embankment and O.G.1. These were the preliminaries to the launch of the second general counter-attack. It was centred on the flanks, in both O.G.1 and O.G.2. In addition, the enemy sent a bombing party down Ostrich Avenue supported by infantry, in the open, close by. Although weakened, the Australians holding O.G.2

repelled the frontal attack as well as the one on the left flank. On the right, however, the counter-attack was more successful. Moving along O.G.2, the attackers linked with men coming down Ostrich Avenue. A valiant stand by Lieutenant P.G.D. Fethers (24th Battalion) was finally brushed aside when Fethers, already wounded, was killed. But time had been gained and the attack was driven back by a combination of artillery and Stokes Mortar shells.

The 62nd Division

The attack by the 62nd Division was assisted by eight tanks of No. 12 Company 'D' Battalion (H.B.M.G.C.). In the report of the actions filed in the War Diary, the Commanding Officer of 'D' Battalion, Lieutenant-Colonel Hardress Lloyd, states that the operational objectives were:

> 'In conjunction with the 62nd Division to capture the village of Bullecourt and hostile system of trenches from U 28.b.88 to U 21 and U 20.b and to advance with the infantry and assist in the capture of Hendecourt.'[3]

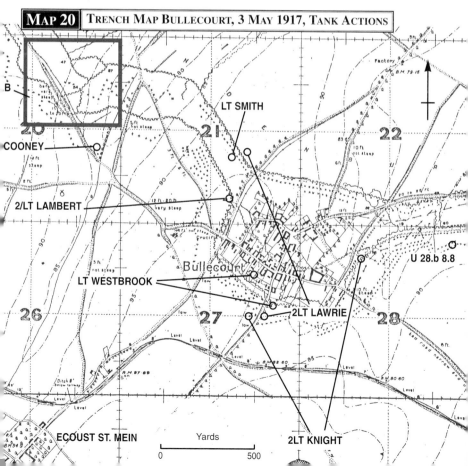

MAP 20 | **TRENCH MAP BULLECOURT, 3 MAY 1917, TANK ACTIONS**

In the event, the objectives were not achieved. In the Official History the failure is attributed to the inability of the infantry to follow the tanks. Hardress Lloyd blames the enemy's use of armour-piercing bullets and the necessity for the tanks to stop. He also considers that the tanks would have been successful if they had managed to keep up with the creeping barrage. As part of the report the fate of each of the eight tanks is shown diagrammatically.

The exact position of the start line is not stated other than to say that it was south of Bullecourt. Zero hour for the tanks was 3.45 a.m., as for the infantry **(See map 20)**.

Tank No. 791

Lieutenant W.S. McCoull entered the village but was lost to view until seen returning at about 5.45 a.m. On the way the tank was hit by a shell and disabled. The crew escaped with their machine guns but later tried to restart the tank. Two further shells hit the tank and nothing further is known of the fate of the crew. Lieutenant McCoull has no known grave and is commemorated on the Memorial to the Missing at Arras.

Tank No. 793

Second Lieutenant C.M. Knight also entered Bullecourt and continued through the village until he encountered the trench running from U.27.b.4.0 to U.28.a.6.7. Finding no infantry beyond the German front line, he patrolled along the trench until forced to retire due to heavy fire from armour-piercing bullets. Four of his crew were

A British tank at Arras, note the snow on the ground. Tank Museum

wounded but, as he retired, he encountered another tank already put out of action. He exchanged his four wounded men for men from the ditched tank and returned to Bullecourt. Finding the front trench no longer occupied he returned to the start line.

Tank No. 598

Second Lieutenant A.R. Lawrie made his way across the Hindenburg Line as far as U.21.d.4.8. By this time he was wounded, as were five of the crew. Of the infantry there was no sign. He had no alternative but to retire but was hit by a shell and put out of action at about U.27.b.5.0 He and his crew made their way to the British lines.

Tank No. 596

Lieutenant T. Westbrook crossed the German front line at 4.10 a.m., and penetrated the enemy ground as far as U.27.b.4.5. Here he met an English officer who asked him to deal with a German machine gun over to the left. Westbrook set off to deal with the gun but, like Knight, was under heavy fire from armour-piercing bullets. He was forced to withdrew via U.27.b.6.2, by which time four of his crew had been wounded. All but one of his guns had been put out of action. He returned to the starting point.

Tank No. 795

Second Lieutenant F.J. Lambert started off 45 minutes after zero hour. On his way to the German line the crew were nearly blinded by the effects of a gas shell which fell very close by. When he reached U.21.d.2.3, he found infantry held up by machine gun fire but could do little as his engine had been damaged and he was losing power. He managed to crawl back to the starting point. He and two of the crew were wounded.

Tank No. 785

Second Lieutenant H.R. Chick started at zero hour and 20 minutes later passed large numbers of infantry streaming back towards their own lines. He pushed on, and came across about 600 men pinned down, in front of the wire, by machine gun fire from a strong point. He stopped and agreed, with the subaltern in charge of the men, to take out the strong point, allowing the infantry to follow up. All went well and he demolished the point but, still the infantry could not advance due to other cross fire. By now four of the crew were casualties and he withdrew.

Tank No. 580

Second Lieutenant R.C. Cooney crossed the German line at about U.20.d.7.8. and mopped up a strong point in U.20.b. He remained at this point for some time but as no support arrived, and with wounded crew members, he returned to the starting point at 7.45 a.m.

The eighth and final tank is also given the Number 795, both in the report and on the diagram, which is an error. Lieutenant E.J. Smith started 45 minutes after zero hour. He reached point U.21.d.3.8 before receiving a direct hit, probably from a German 5.9. Three of the crew were wounded and the tank set on fire. The team managed to evacuate the tank and, having seen them on their way back to safety, Smith returned to the tank and managed to douse the fire. Although himself wounded, he got the tank back to the starting point by about 8.00 a.m.

No explanation is given in the diary for the late start by two of the tanks. In a *Company of Tanks*, Major W.H.L. Watson asserts that all tanks started on time.

The orders received by the 62nd Division on 27 April for the attack on 3 May specified that, in addition to the capture of the villages of Bullecourt and Hendecourt, it was to take the length of O.G.2 between U.22.d.0.3. and U.14.d.3.0. Further, once in Hendecourt, it was to set up a defensive flank from west of the village to point U.20.a.9.6. in O.G.2 **(See map 21)**. The attack, to be carried out simultaneously with those by the 1st Anzac Corps and the British Third Army, was to be launched from a position to the south and west of Bullecourt.

Diagram showing the fate of the tanks involved in 3 May attack, at Bullecourt, as recorded in the unit war diary. Tank Museum

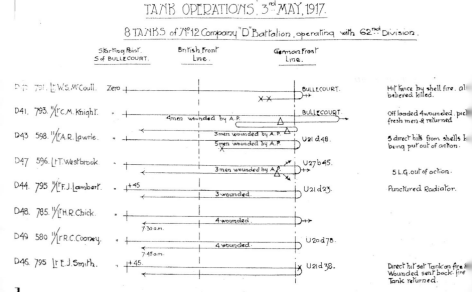

The division was to use all three of its brigades: the 185th Brigade on the right, the 186th Brigade in the centre and the 187th Brigade on the left. To the 185th Brigade was assigned the task of capturing Bullecourt, including the front and support trenches of the Hindenburg Line, from U.22.d.0.3. to U.21.d.5.5. The 186th Brigade was to secure the front and support trenches on its front and then to push on to capture Hendecourt. The 187th Brigade was to form the defensive flank. To effect the capture of Bullecourt, the 185th Brigade was to use the two battalions of the West Yorkshire Regiment, the 2/6 Battalion on the right and the 2/5 Battalion on the left. The 2/7 Battalion was in support but the 2/8 Battalion had been lent to the 186th Brigade. Two battalions were deemed sufficient to capture Bullecourt! In the centre, four battalions of the Duke of Wellington's Regiment were deployed: the 2/5 Battalion on the right and the 2/6 Battalion on the left, with the 2/7 Battalion and 2/4 Battalion respectively, in the rear. The 'borrowed' battalion of the West Yorkshire was further back still. On the left of the divisional front, the 187th Brigade had two battalions of the York and Lancaster Regiment in the line: the 2/4 Battalion on the right and the 2/5 Battalion on the left. The 2/5 KOYLI, with two companies of the 2/4 KOYLI, were in the rear of the two front line battalions The remaining two companies of the 2/4 KOYLI were in the rear of the 2/5 Battalion. The situation at the start of the action is described in the history of the Division:

'Shortly after two o'clock in the morning the moon disappeared and the night turned to inky blackness, but fifteen minutes before Zero all was ready for the attack. At this period the enemy put down a very heavy barrage on the 185th Infantry Brigade, which gradually spread along the whole front.

At Zero the creeping barrage opened on the enemy's position and the assaulting troops began to move forward immediately. But now an unexpected difficulty presented itself: the warm weather had baked the ground hard and as the shells fell, churning it up, clouds of dust filled the air, and with the smoke from the guns, and the smoke bombs, objectives were hidden from the advancing troops and there was much loss of direction.' [4]

The story of the attack, on all fronts, was one of mixed success and failure.

185th Brigade

The 2/5 West Yorkshire found the wire well cut and, quickly captured O.G.1 and pressed on into the village, where it established

APPROXIMATE LINE

Ground to the west of Bullecourt from which the British 62nd Division attacked.

two posts. However, the 2/6 West Yorkshire was less fortunate. It was badly cut up by machine gun fire and, in the confusion and smoke, veered off line. Large numbers of men from the battalion, both dead and wounded, were later found in front of the German wire. By about 7.00 a.m., more posts had been set up including one at the objective U.21.d.5.5. The whole of O.G.1 had been occupied as far as the junction with the trench running south from the Crucifix where contact existed with the 2/5 Duke of Wellington's of 186th Brigade. The fate of the 2/6 Battalion was unclear. All attempts, including one by the 2/7 West Yorkshire, to make contact failed. The 2/7 was met by such murderous machine gun fire that it was forced to retire to the shelter of the railway.

186th Brigade

The 2/5 Duke of Wellington's also found the wire well cut. They entered O.G.1 and established a line from U.21.d.1.0 to U.21.d.2.4 where they were later reinforced by men of the 2/8 West Yorkshire. Meanwhile the 2/6 Duke of Wellington's found the wire uncut and were held up and ultimately forced to seek cover in some of the many shell-holes.

187th Brigade

On the left flank the 2/5 York and Lancaster reached its first objective without difficulty but the 2/4 Battalion was caught up on very thick wire entanglements. In an endeavour to find a way around

Line of the railway embankment in front of Ecoust-St-Mein.

the wire, the attackers moved to their left and became mixed with the 2/5 Battalion. Further problems ensued when the 2/5 KOYLI, attempting to follow up, lost their commanding officer Colonel W. Watson while attempting to rally his troops. His body was never recovered and he is commemorated on the Memorial to the Missing at Arras.

At 6.50 a.m. the situation was so confused that it was decided that the protective barrage should be maintained on the second objective until a further advance could be organised. Repeated attempts, later in the morning, by the 186th and 187th Brigades to make ground were beaten back. The remnants of the 2/5 Duke of Wellington's and the 2/8 West Yorkshire were bombed out of their portion of trench and driven back into open ground where they took shelter in shell-holes. By mid-day the 2/5 West Yorkshire had been driven out of Bullecourt and had taken cover on the line of the railway, along with the 2/7 West Yorkshire. Of the 2/6 West Yorkshire there was no news. Units of the

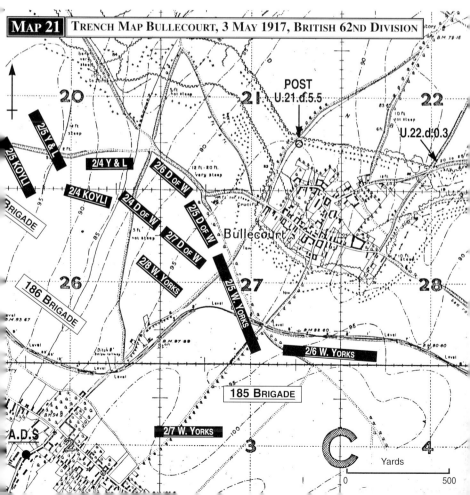

MAP 21 TRENCH MAP BULLECOURT, 3 MAY 1917, BRITISH 62ND DIVISION

186th Brigade were either back on the line of the railway or sheltering in the sunken road near the forming-up positions. The 187th Brigade was in the same sunken road or in shell-holes adjacent to it.

By 5.00 p.m. it was clear that the division had failed in its attempt to capture Bullecourt and was in no state to renew the attack. Orders were sent to the Brigade commanders to reorganise their battalions on their original fronts. At the same time the 185th Brigade was told to be prepare to hand over to the 7th Division as soon as possible. The reasons for the failure are summed up by the divisional historian:

> 'The failure of the 62nd Division to capture Bullecourt was due largely to a fault which certainly cannot be charged to the gallant troops who stormed the village and the Hindenburg Line in the vicinity. Neither could the Divisional Staff, which had laboured to make all the arrangements as complete as possible, be blamed. It was due principally to an error in tactics which had so often failed in the earlier years of the war - notably at Festubert in 1915. The Australian Division on the right of the 62nd Division did not launch its attack side by side with the 2/6th West Yorks., the flanking battalion of the West Riding Division. There was a gap - a fatal gap - in the line of attack between the Colonials and the Yorkshiremen. ...Thus some hundred of yards of the enemy's positions (unfortunately that portion which was very strongly defended by machine guns) was left free to enfilade the 2/6th West Yorks. as that battalion advanced: which indeed happened. In all justice to the Australian troops it must be noted that they reached their objective, but before they got there the West Yorkshiremen had been cut up and of those brave fellows who had penetrated the village the greater number had either been killed, wounded or taken prisoner, only a hundred survivors getting back to their own trenches.
>
> The inky blackness of the night, which caused much confusion during the forming-up operations, also contributed to the failure of the assault, many of the troops losing themselves and being entirely ignorant of the direction of the enemy's trenches.'[5]

On 3 May, the 62nd Division lost 116 officers and 2,860 other ranks, killed, wounded and missing.

Consequent upon the failures of the Australian 5th Brigade and the British 62nd Division either side of the Australian 6th Brigade, changes were made in the artillery timings. The programme was put back to give the 5th Brigade time to catch up. Instead of leaving the second objective at 6.00 a.m., it was delayed until 6.30 a.m. Gellibrand, conscious of the exposed position of his troops, requested that the advance of the 6th Brigade also be delayed. This request was initially turned down by V Corps. When it became known that Bullecourt had not been captured and that the protective artillery cover on their second objective was to be retained, Birdwood ordered that the Australians should remain on the second objective and delay any further advance until the 62nd Division was in a position to assist.

In an attempt to rectify flank failures, General Smyth decided to use two battalions of the 7th Brigade. He ordered the 25th Battalion to assault Bullecourt village from the south-east, from a position on the railway embankment **(See map 18)**. The commanding officer, Lieutenant-Colonel E.C. Norrie, mindful of the exposed nature of the ground over which the attack was to take place, decided to employ only two platoons in the first instance. These moved out from the railway shortly after 7.00 a.m., but when some 300 yards from the village were stopped by withering machine gun fire. They took cover in nearby shell-holes from which only half their number returned under the cover of darkness. The attack was reported as a failure. The second battalion of the 7th Brigade, the 26th, was ordered to move up under the cover provided by the semi-sunken Central Road to assist the 5th Brigade in O.G.1. They were employed for the remainder of the day, as carrying parties bringing up bombs, rifle-grenades and mortars. As the fighting for O.G.1 went back and forth, the remnants of the 6th Brigade in O.G.2 were also being hard pressed. At about 8.00 a.m. they were pushed right back to the junction of O.G.2 with Central Road, whereupon Captain Pascoe moved down from his position near the Six Cross Roads to barricade the trench at the junction. The situation was critical and remained so until a trench mortar was brought up from O.G.1 which succeeded in driving the enemy back to Ostrich Avenue.

It was 2.00 p.m. before the 28th Battalion moved up Central Road with orders to attack both the trenches of the Hindenburg Line. In command of the 28th Battalion was Lieutenant-Colonel G.A. Read, a remarkable man who in 22 months had risen from the rank of private to that of Lieutenant-Colonel. The attack on O.G.1 was led by Major A. Brown and that on O.G.2 by Captain A.M.P. Montgomery, each attack employing two companies **(See map 22)**. In O.G.2, the attackers were stopped by machine gun fire from cross-trench "F" and from the Riencourt-Noreuil road behind it. Eventually, they were forced to retire to a barricade near cross-trench "G". The simultaneous attack in O.G.1 was, according to Bean, a brilliant success:

'*Covered by a Stokes mortar - which, however, eventually had* *to be stopped through its erratic shooting - and by four Lewis guns stationed on the bank of Central Road, the Western Australians advanced, seizing two bays of the trench at each rush. The corps observer, telephoning to corps headquarters from the spur beyond Noreuil, reported that he could see bombers working in the open, rushing with great spirit along the parapet. After the attack had progressed 100 yards, an additional Lewis gun was placed out in a shell-hole south of O.G.1, to cover the further advance. The Germans were quickly driven as far as cross-trench "F", and the mouth of this was next captured and barricaded; but beyond that point the enemy's resistance stiffened.'* [6]*

At 4.00 p.m., the Germans counter-attacked and by 5.30 p.m. the Australians had been driven back to Central Road. Here Major Brown rallied his men and, helped by the arrival of a fresh supply of bombs, renewed the attack. By 6.00 p.m. the men of the 28th were back at the Riencourt-Noreuil road, some 400 yards from Central Road, only to be ejected yet again at 8.15 p.m.

During the day news reached the Australian divisional and brigade commanders that the British 7th Division was to take over from the British 62nd Division. It would renew the attack on Bullecourt in the evening, and then endeavour to advance to the second objective. Accordingly, the Australians were to be ready to move to their second objective at the same time. The 6th Brigade was in no state to comply with these orders and, when this was pointed out by Gellibrand to General Smyth, he agreed to a modified scheme. In this, the 6th Brigade was required to use the 23rd and 24th Battalions to bomb down to the cross-trench "L", by 6.00 p.m. If the proposed advance was possible, it would be executed by two fresh battalions from the reserve. Even as preparations were being made by the two battalions, the Germans launched a third counter-attack, mainly on the right flank, which, although repulsed, further reduced the numbers. As the light began to fail, yet another set of orders was issued by General Smyth:

'The trenches were to be held - on the right by the 28th Battalion and the 5th Brigade, and on the left by the 6th Brigade. The latter was to co-operate with the 7th British Division's attack, but would be relieved in O.G.2 before midnight by two battalions of the 1st Brigade, which, with the 5th Brigade, would advance to the second objective when the 7th Division did so.' [7]

Again, before action could be taken, the Germans took a hand. As already noted, the 28th Battalion was ejected from its position in O.G.1

and a heavy barrage was laid down on the ground behind the Hindenburg Line. A retaliatory barrage fell short, as had happened earlier in the day, and some men of the 6th Brigade were forced to retire from O.G.2 in the vicinity of its junction with Diagonal Road. As these men streamed down Central Road, Major Brown of the 28th Battalion assumed that his position was no longer tenable and ordered the retirement of the battalion along with the remnants of the 5th Brigade. However, the remainder of the 6th Brigade hung on in O.G.1 and O.G.2 and on both flanks. At 1.00 a.m. on 4 May there began to arrive the first companies of the relieving 1st and 3rd Battalions of the Australian 1st Brigade (1st Division). The worn-out troops of the 6th Brigade were able to retire down the newly-completed communication trench, Pioneer Trench (Avenue) which ran along Central Road. As the relief was taking place, the Germans delivered yet another counter-

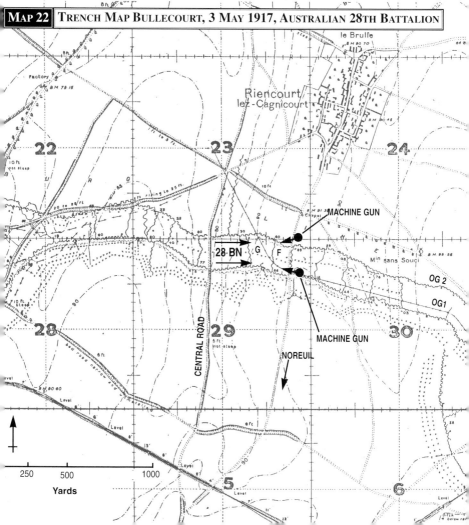

MAP 22 | **TRENCH MAP BULLECOURT, 3 MAY 1917, AUSTRALIAN 28TH BATTALION**

attack, their fourth. They struck at both the right and left flanks but were beaten back by the fresh troops, aided by the remnants of the 6th Brigade and the 3rd Battalion which had just started to relieve the 5th Brigade.

The 7th Division

The 7th Division

It was the 22nd Brigade (7th Division), which was given the task of capturing Bullecourt after the failure of the 62nd Division. The brigade moved into Mory on 2 May with orders to be ready to support the coming attack if necessary. Two battalions, the 1/RWF and the 2/HAC, were in Mory, with the two remaining battalions, the 2/Royal Warwicks and the 20/Manchesters, at L'Homme Mort south of Ecoust-St.-Mein and Mory Copse respectively. When the attack by the 62nd Division was underway, the 2/Royal Warwicks and the 20/Manchesters were ordered up to positions on the railway embankment south of Bullecourt, the remaining two battalions moving up from Mory to replace them. At around mid-day, the decision was taken to use the brigade to replace the 62nd Division. It was ordered to attack Bullecourt with two battalions, the first objective being a line running south-east to north-west through the northern part of the village **(See Map 23)**. The final objective was the Hindenburg Line to the north of the village (Bovis Trench). The plan required the attack to be launched by the 1/RWF and the 2/HAC, who would move up through the lines of the two battalions on the embankment. If the first objective was secured, the 20/Manchesters and the 2/Royal Warwicks would then move up to the second objective. The assault was at first scheduled for 6.30 p.m., but later delayed until 10.30 p.m. As has already been noted, the Australian attack scheduled for the same time did not take place.

In daylight, the 1/RWF and the 2/HAC took their places on the embankment, opposite Tower Trench, the name given to the section of trench running around the south face of Bullecourt, and waited for zero hour. The attack is described in the Divisional History:

> *'Their advance had apparently been detected by the Germans, for directly they went forward heavy machine gun fire opened upon them from front and flank; they pressed forward nevertheless, only to find the wire, though effectively cut, still presented a troublesome obstacle, being tangled up in coils which were difficult to negotiate. However, both battalions succeeded in forcing their way into Tower Trench, and cleared it after a stubborn hand-to-hand tussle, capturing about 50 prisoners. Some of the later waves of the HAC pressed forward into the village and were even reported to have reached the*

98

second objective, while the Welch Fusiliers tried to form a defensive flank facing north-west...there was a gap to the right; it appeared later that the Australian battalion which should have co-operated had suffered so severely from a heavy bombardment that it had had to be relieved, and in consequence Germans, making use of this gap, assailed the HAC in flank. The HAC put up a good fight, but they had Germans in front and in flank and even some behind, who had come out of dugouts that had escaped the moppers-up. The Welch Fusiliers were not less severely pressed, and in the end neither they nor the HAC could maintain their hold on Bullecourt: by 2.30 a.m. on May 4th, it was reported that both battalions had been thrust out of the village. Accordingly instead of the Warwickshires and the 20th Manchesters starting the second stage of the attack at 2 a.m., they had to be put in at 3 a.m. to repeat the first phase. As they were forming up they were caught by the German barrage and lost heavily: the 20th Manchesters indeed were much scattered and disorganised, and Colonel Smalley could not collect enough of them to make much of an attack. It was 4 a.m. before the attack could be launched, and it was hardly surprising, seeing how

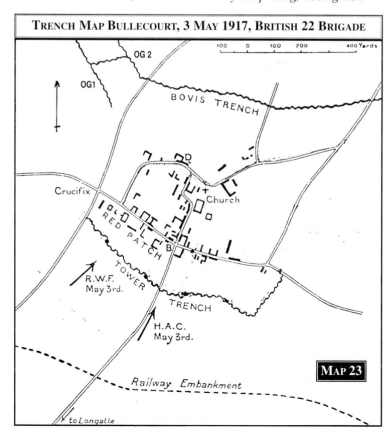

TRENCH MAP BULLECOURT, 3 MAY 1917, BRITISH 22 BRIGADE

MAP 23

badly both units had suffered from the barrage, that they hardly fared even as well as their predecessors. The Royal Warwickshires started quite well: like the Welch Fusiliers they got into the front trench and even penetrated into the village only to be dislodged by counter-attacks. The majority of the survivors fell back to the embankment, but about 50 men with 3 officers managed to hold on in Tower Trench where it crossed the Longatte road and a company of the Manchesters got in further to the right, S.E. of the village. During the day various conflicting reports came through...not till the early afternoon was the situation more or less cleared up as a result of a reconnaissance by Captain Hunter of the Brigade staff. His report showed that about 80 Welch Fusiliers were inside the German wire near the Crucifix but had not reached the front trench: the party of the Royal Warwickshires astride the Longatte road was still holding on, but that was all. The front trench, though full of dead, both British and German, appeared to be unoccupied. The HAC, except for a few men still on the railway embankment, were back near Ecoust reorganising, the 20th Manchesters were doing the same near Ecoust station; but losses had been heavy and the 22nd Brigade was in no condition to repeat the attack.' [8]

A final attempt to occupy Bullecourt was made by the 2/Royal Warwicks and the 1/RWF in the early evening. That it was forced back by heavy machine gun fire showed that the enemy was still firmly in control of the village.

The 1st Brigade

By the morning of 4 May, the troops holding the Australian positions were all members of the 1st Brigade. However, they were under the orders of the commanders of the 5th and 6th Brigades, Brigadiers Smith and Gellibrand. To the left of Central Road, Gellibrand now commanded the 1st and 3rd Battalions; and to the right of the road Smith commanded the 2nd Battalion with the promise of the 4th Battalion. In the words of Bean, the operations on 4 May were designed to 'gain elbow-room'**(See map 24)**. The 1st and 3rd Battalions sent bombing parties down O.G.1 and O.G.2 respectively. After fierce fighting, in which they were aided by mortars of the 6th Brigade, they reached cross-trench "L", some 700 yards from Central Road. The corresponding attack on the right flank was delayed while arrangements for artillery cover were completed. The 2nd Battalion finally entered O.G.1 and O.G.2 at 2.15 p.m., 75 minutes after the attack by the 1st and 3rd Battalions. Immediately some gains were made in both trenches, but so stiff was the German resistance in the vicinity of cross-trench "G" that a halt was called and the position subjected to an artillery barrage. Following the barrage, the bombing was renewed and a fierce contest developed between the deadly British Mills grenades, and the longer range, but less effective, German egg and stick-grenades. As the afternoon wore on, the 4th Battalion started to file up Pioneer Trench and into the two Hindenburg Lines. Although not ordered to take part in the attack, they immediately joined the fray and continued the advance. By evening the fighting died down. The Australians were left in control of O.G.1 up to a point just east of cross-trench "F" and O.G.2 to a point just in front of the same cross-trench. They had gained about 800 yards and were at the same point as the

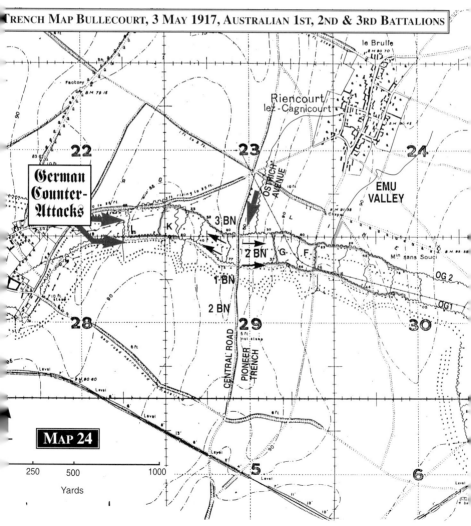

TRENCH MAP BULLECOURT, 3 MAY 1917, AUSTRALIAN 1ST, 2ND & 3RD BATTALIONS

28th Battalion the day before, the difference being that this time they had sufficient men and ammunition to hold their line.

As ever, the Germans were not content to accept the losses. At about 7.00 p.m., they started a two-hour bombardment which covered the whole area in front of the railway embankment and the captured portions of O.G.1 and O.G.2. This was the overture to the fifth counter-attack, which involved attacks down Ostrich Avenue and from Diagonal Road in the vicinity of cross-trench "L". The former was easily beaten back by machine gun and rifle fire, but the enemy succeeded in regaining O.G.2 as far as cross-trench "K", from the 3rd Battalion, leaving the 1st Battalion still in O.G.1 as far as cross-trench "L".

By the early morning of 5 May, significant changes had been made in the composition and disposition of the Australian forces holding the Hindenburg Line. The whole of the 1st Brigade had been moved to the left side of Central Road. The 1st and 3rd Battalions occupied O.G.2 and O.G.1 respectively, with the 2nd and 4th Battalions in reserve. Brigadier Gellibrand was relieved by the commander of the 1st Brigade, Lieutenant-Colonel I. Mackay. On the right, the 11th and 12th Battalions were side by side in both O.G.1 and O.G.2, the 11th adjacent to Central Road and the 12th on the right flank. The 2nd and 4th Battalions were in reserve. Brigadier Smith was relieved by the commander of the 3rd Brigade, Lieutenant-Colonel L.M. Mullen.*

Extract from a memoir written by Private B Harris C Company 2nd Battalion AIF:

> 'At 12.30 the next morning 5th May, we moved up the trench we had dug to support the 2nd Division. We remained in this trench until midday on 5th when we moved into the German line. We bombed along this trench using rifle grenades and when our supply of these was exhausted, had taken some eighty yards of trench. At this point it was decided to erect a bomb-stop across the trench and while this was being done, a Lewis gun was posted on the near bank of the trench. ...Almost immediately the Germans commenced a counter-attack, as we were out of rifle grenades, they succeeded in driving us back about fifty yards. However, rifle grenades again being supplied, we once more drove the enemy back. He made several attempts to dislodge us, once a number appeared on No Man's Land and by the signs they were making it was believed that they wished to surrender. We waved them in but when they arrived at a point about 20 yards from our trench they dropped into shell-holes and gave us

*Both Brigadiers were on leave in England.

a plastering with potato-mashers (stick bombs). Despite this, they did not succeed in entering the trench although our numbers had been greatly reduced by casualties.

When this attack failed, our attention was directed to the environs of Quéant. Here a considerable number collected and commenced moving towards us. They did not, however, get very far as they presented an excellent machine gun target. After sunset the battle quietened down which was just as well for us, as we had only about one fifth of our original number. About midnight the few of us who had survived were relieved by the 12th Battalion.'

Preparations were now in hand for the 3rd Brigade to push the line eastwards. It was intended that the 11th and 12th Battalions should change places, permitting the 11th to lead the assault. However, during the day the enemy laid down two very heavy barrages, which produced numerous casualties, leaving the brigade in no state to attack. During the night of 5/6 May, the enemy's artillery again blasted O.G.1, O.G.2, Pioneer Trench and the railway embankment. Men of the 12th Battalion, nearest the enemy, escaped, but the remainder of both battalions suffered further losses. At 5.00 a.m., a counter-attack was launched from two directions: westwards along both O.G.1 and O.G.2; and southwards in, and adjacent to, Ostrich Avenue. The attack, near Ostrich Avenue, was quickly broken up. By coincidence, it started at the exact time at which an artillery barrage, in support of the proposed 3rd Brigade attack, had been scheduled. Although, the infantry assault had been abandoned, the artillery support had not been cancelled. It stopped the Germans in their tracks! In O.G.2 the Germans managed

The point where O.G. 1 crossed Central Road and Corporal Howell won the Victoria Cross.

to gain some 40 yards of trench but in O.G.1 the situation soon became serious. Led by two *flammenwerfer* they pushed the defenders back to the junction of O.G.1 with Central Road. Here the advance was halted by the combined efforts of two machine guns: one in Central Road and a second firing from cross-trench "G". As the Germans gathered their forces to renew the onslaught, men of the 1st Battalion crossed Central Road to bolster the defences. One of these, Corporal G.J. Howell, jumped out of the trench and ran along the side of O.G.1 throwing bombs on to the Germans until he was finally wounded and fell. For this action, which led to the withdrawal of the enemy, he was awarded the Victoria Cross. With this magnificent lead, the Australians rallied and followed the retiring Germans, driving them out of both O.G. Lines, regaining all the lost ground.

It was now recognised by both the brigade and divisional commanders that further progress eastwards was unlikely. They decided to seal off both O.G. trenches by filling in several bays and wiring the ground in front of cross-trench "F". This task was carried out during the night of 6/7 May by a working party of engineers under Lieutenant F.S. Scarr. Unfortunately, as they withdrew having completed the work in O.G.1, Scarr and several of his men were killed, leaving O.G.2 untouched. This failure was to be responsible for the enemy gaining entrance to O.G.2 during the counter-attack on 15 May. The omission was rectified once the counter-attack had been repulsed.

On 7 May a further attempt was made, by the British 7th Division, to capture Bullecourt. Following its failure on 3 May, the 22nd Brigade, which had lost heavily, was withdrawn from the line and replaced by the 20th Brigade (Brigadier-General H.R. Green). The new attack was to be delivered by the 2/Gordon Highlanders and the 9/Devons from the south-east with three objectives **(See map 25)**. Two companies of the 2/Gordons were to lead, followed by two companies of the 9/Devons, the latter to consolidate the first objective or 'Blue Line', part of O.G.1, Tower Trench, running in front of Bullecourt. The 2/Gordons were then to be joined by the rear two companies to push on

The ground, in front of Bullecourt, known as the 'Red Patch'.

to the second objective or 'Green Line' which included the south-east corner of the village and ran roughly north-east to link up with the Australians. The third objective or 'Brown Line' ran along the road around the northern part of the village. A substantial portion of the village was not to be attacked. This was the 'Red Patch', so called because it was coloured red on trench maps. It would, however, be under constant shell fire during the attack and taken later in the day, if conditions allowed. Two companies of the 8/Devons held the ground to the south of the village, either side of the Longatte road, along the railway embankment.

Zero hour was 3.45 a.m., at which time the Gordons passed through the wire and stormed the German line. The Blue Line was taken and, as planned, the Gordons pressed on to the Green Line leaving the Devons to consolidate in Tower Trench. By 6.00 a.m. the second objective had been captured along with a substantial number of prisoners. A message was send back, to the effect that bombers had moved eastwards and linked up with the Australians. The German artillery now began to pound the remains of Bullecourt. The Gordons were forced to abandoned parts of the Green Line but held fast in Tower Trench. So encouraged was the divisional commander, General T.H. Shoubridge, that he ordered Brigadier Green to use the 9/Devons to clear the Red Patch, by working westward

Continued fighting at Bullecourt, Anzacs in Hindenburg Line. The Daily Telegraph, Monday 7 May 1917.

ANZACS IN HINDENBURG LINE.

HEADQUARTERS (France), Sunday.

The chief feature of the fighting during the past twenty-four hours has once again been the continuance of the German counter-attacks in the immediate vicinity of Bullecourt, and the wonderful tenacity with which, in defiance of these, the Anzac troops maintain and steadily extend their hold upon the Hindenburg Line east of that place. The fighting here appears to have become a great bombing match, in which the individuality of the Australian soldiers has proved much superior to the machine-like methods of the Hun.

Within the Bullecourt enclave the struggle continues to ebb and flow, and for the moment the German machine-gun fire seems to dominate the ruined village. But our artillery is continuously combing the place and rendering the enemy's tenure so costly that it would be all in our favour, if he should go on putting in fresh troops in the endeavour to try to hold it. Our line follows the outskirts of the village around three sides, and as our gunners have observation across the fourth side, the position is not a particularly good one for the Germans.

The Australians appear now to hold a considerable length of the Hindenburg Line, and the bombing parties, working as a rule behind a shrapnel barrage, which very slowly creeps forward and assists in clearing up the trench ahead, are steadily increasing their gain. That the Boches view with much concern the successful invasion of this much-vaunted defence is best proven by the numerous and desperate efforts they are making to retover the position. Since Thursday morning the Anzacs have had to deal with no less than thirteen distinct counter-attacks, all in force, and one of them at least dealt from four directions simultaneously. But every one of these attempts has been defeated, and the enemy losses have been very heavy. In their confusion they have been seen both firing into and bombing their own people, one of these cases being an attempt at surprise by a large body of Boches who emerged from a deep dug-out, to be headed off and blown up by another party of Boches, who had evidently been reduced to a condition of jumpiness by the Anzacs.

Taking occasion by the hand, the "Wallabies" followed the dispersal of one of these attacks by the artillery—for whose work, by the way, they have nothing but the highest praise—by a counterattack, and got into a trench in which they found two minenwerfer emplanted, with a large supply of ammunition dumped ready to hand, which they proceeded to return to its rightful owners with great gusto. During these operations they have rounded in considerably over 100 prisoners, including one officer of the typically arrogant Prussian caste. The fact that most of the prisoners taken are from the 3rd Guards Division and the 2nd Guards Reserve suggests that the enemy is throwing in some of his best troops opposite to the Anzacs.—*Reuter's Special Service.*

along Tower Trench. By 1.00 p.m., the Gordons had crossed the Longatte Road and were within reach of the north-west corner of the Red Patch. In this advance they rescued a handful of the 2/HAC who had been holed up in the village since 3 May.

At 3.30 p.m. the inevitable German counter-attack was launched. Large numbers of the enemy were seen advancing from the north west.

Major-General T.H. Shoubridge CB, CMG, DSO, GOC British 7th Division during operations at Bullecourt.

Although hindered by artillery fire they managed to enter the Red Patch and drove the weakened Gordons back to a point just in front of the Green Line. During the night the Gordons in the Green Line were relieved by 2/Borders. and two companies of the 8/Devons replaced two of the 9/Devons in the Blue Line. At 11 a.m. the following morning, the 8/Devons renewed the assault on the Red Patch. Initial success was followed by stubborn resistance and counter-attack. By evening, the Devons were only just in front of the 'Green Line'. The 2/Borders, meanwhile, were heavily shelled for most of the day but managed to hold on. That night the remaining companies of the 8/Devons relieved those of the 9/Devons still holding part of the Blue Line.

General Shoubridge was now adamant that Bullecourt could and should be cleared. Accordingly, at mid-day on 9 May, the 8/Devons renewed the attack. As in the previous attacks,

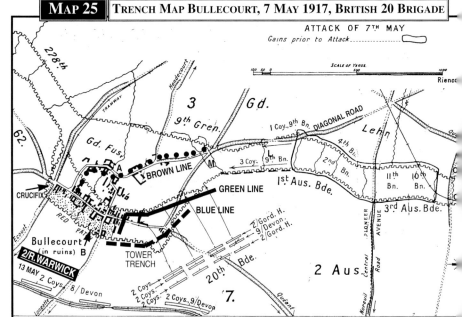

MAP 25 | **TRENCH MAP BULLECOURT, 7 MAY 1917, BRITISH 20 BRIGADE**

bombers led the way, followed by rifle-grenade men and Lewis gunners covered by trench mortars. Machine guns were positioned on the railway embankment to sweep the ground to the north of the village to hamper movement of German reinforcements. As soon as the attack started the Devons were subjected to a heavy German barrage. In spite of this they made ground, particularly on the right, before being driven back. They rallied and, with some reinforcements, attacked again, driving the enemy into open ground where he was caught in fire from the machine guns on the railway embankment. By late afternoon, the Devons had established a secure line, just east of the Longatte road, a gain of about 100 yards. The brigade was progressively relieved by the 91st Brigade (Brigadier-General H.R. Cumming). The results are summed up by the Divisional historian:

> 'The 20th Brigade, with 11 officers and 157 men killed and missing, 25 officers and 568 men wounded, had suffered nearly as much as the 22nd, the loss falling heaviest on the 8/Devons and the Gordons, the Borders and 9/Devons getting off comparatively lightly with about 130 casualties apiece. The brigade had the satisfaction of having secured a firm hold on the south-eastern portion of Bullecourt and having taken a heavy toll of the Germans, but there was something unsatisfactory and depressing in these piecemeal attacks, repeated over the same ground and without substantial alterations of plan to hold out to each succeeding attack prospects of better fortune than had attended its predecessors.' [9]

That the Germans had suffered badly was evidenced by a lull in the fighting which continued for two days.

The 2/Queen's and 1/South Staffs, 91st Brigade, relieved the 20th Brigade on 10 May. The Queen's were deployed on the right and the South Staffs on the left. The 22/Manchesters were in support, at Ecoust and on the railway embankment, whilst the 21/Manchesters were held in the rear. On the evening of 11 May tapes were laid to the east of the Longatte road in preparation for a fresh attack. The objective was the Brown Line of earlier attacks and the attack was to be carried out by two companies each of the Queen's and South Staffs. A creeping barrage was to advance at a rate of 100 yards in six minutes. Subsidiary attacks would be carried out by the Australians and by the British 62nd Division, the latter division assaulting a strong point at the Crucifix in Bullecourt.

At 3.40 a.m. on 12 May the two battalions went forward. On the right the Queen's moved through the village and by 4.15 a.m. were consolidating a position in front of the road marking the Brown Line. They had suffered few casualties and set up several machine guns in positions to stem any counter-attacks. On the other flank the South Staffs were not so fortunate. Caught in a German barrage, and fire from the Red Patch, the attack south of the road towards the Crucifix was soon held up. North of the road, the advance was more successful. Some men managed to reach point A near the site of the church at the same time making contact with the Queens. However, the bulk of the battalion was stopped by a machine gun, at point B, which forced it to take up a curved line to the west of the cross-roads. The presence of the machine gun in the Red Patch prevented reserves being introduced until after dark. At 3.40 a.m. on the following day, the attack was renewed by two companies of the 22/Manchesters, in place of the South Staffs, and a battalion on loan from the 22nd Brigade. This battalion, the 2/Royal Warwicks, was deployed south of Bullecourt, on a line, between the roads to Longatte and the Crucifix. It was ordered to clear the Red Patch while the Manchesters attacked in the east. Unfortunately, the Germans had decided to hold Tower Trench in some strength, so that very few of the 2/Royal Warwicks even managed to get beyond the wire. A similar fate befell the 22/Manchesters who, like the South Staffs before them, were pinned down by machine guns in

Australian troops with a Stokes mortar in the Hindenburg Line. 8 May 1917. IWM E(Aus). 457

the Red Patch and near the cross-roads. Still the orders remained 'Bullecourt must be taken'. A weakened HAC was ordered to relieve the South Staffs and the Royal Welch Fusiliers were also brought up for another attack. The Queen's, who were still in position, now found that the Australians had been taken out of the line on 12 May to be replaced by the 173rd Brigade of the British 58th Division.

The new assault by the 1/RWF was made up of two operations. Two companies attacked the south-west side of the village at 2.10 a.m. on 14 May and established posts in Tower Trench: one at its junction with the road to the Crucifix and the other about 100 yards further east. At 6.15 a.m. the remaining companies attacked from the south-east, supported by fire from the two posts. A very fierce fight ensued with the 1/RWF suffering heavy casualties before becoming bogged down where the Longatte road entered the village. If they could have been supplied with ammunition there was a strong possibility that they could have succeeded in finally taking the whole of the Red Patch and the remains of the village. Unfortunately, supplies ran out at the same time as the enemy counter-attacked and all the ground gained was lost.

58th Division

All units of the 91st Brigade were now tired and weak but a final effort was still required of them. The 20/Manchesters took over the line from the junction with the 173rd Brigade to the site of the church, the 2/HAC continued to the left north of the 'Red Patch' and the 21/Manchesters were in a number of isolated positions around the southern and eastern edges of the village. The changes had hardly been completed when the Germans counter-attacked. The 2/HAC was attacked from the Crucifix and driven back until it managed to hold in Tower Trench and establish a line running from the church to the cross-roads. The 20/Manchesters and the 173rd Brigade managed to hold the enemy but the situation became very confused. The two companies of the 1/RWF, who had participated in the second of their battalion's attacks, were preparing to attack again when the German onslaught commenced. They moved up to the cross-roads and helped to prevent the Germans crossing the Longatte road. This road then constituted the left half of the line which the 91st Brigade handed over on the night of 15/16 May.

> '*The Division was certainly sadly reduced when at 10 a.m. on May 16th General Shoubridge handed over command to the G.O.C. Fifty-Eight Division. The 20th Brigade reported that it could produce three battalions of about 450 men apiece and one of 250; the 22nd, whose units had another 350 casualties while in action under the 91st, could only muster about 800 men; and*

Mory Abbey Cemetery, Mory.

the 91st, which had lost 700 of all ranks, was in little better plight. ...Bullecourt cost the Division 128 officers and 2,554 men, 40 officers and 879 men being killed or missing.' [10]

Among the officers killed was Lieutenant-Colonel J.H. Chadwick, commanding the 24th Manchester (Pioneers). He is buried in Mory Abbey Cemetery, Mory.

In preparation for the 7th Division attacks, General Shoubridge asked General Smyth for Australian support in securing his right flank. He requested that an effort be made to capture O.G.1 and O.G.2 up to the north-east corner of Bullecourt. The troops holding the line in the vicinity of the proposed attack, the 3rd Battalion, were too exhausted to carry on so the task was allotted to the 9th Battalion. During the afternoon of 6 May, the 1st and 3rd Battalions were taken out of the O.G.1 and O.G.2 and replaced by the 4th and 2nd Battalions. In the evening, the 9th Battalion joined them, putting three companies in O.G.1, the site of the major attack and one in O.G.2. **(See map 25)**. At 4.00 a.m. the leading platoon set off down the foremost German trench. After about 70 yards, it was met by a shower of bombs and, after a fierce exchange, forced to withdraw. On seeing their comrades forced back, the next platoon went forward with rifle grenades which they fired over the defenders to prevent fresh supplies of bombs being brought up to them. Lewis gunners clambered out of the trench and took positions in shell-holes to fire on the Germans. Eventually, the volume of bombs coming from the enemy lines lessened and, heartened by this, the Australians renewed their efforts. They were rewarded by seeing Germans fleeing down cross-trench "M" to O.G.2. At 5.15 a.m. they made contact with Captain M.L. Gordon of the 2/Gordon Highlanders.

In O.G.2 the intention was to move forward as far as the junction of the trench with the cross-roads. At 4.00 a.m. the leading two platoons climbed up out of the trench, and moved along each side of Diagonal

Road. They almost reached cross-trench "L" before being held up. Here they were joined by the two remaining platoons and, together, they drove the enemy out of the cross-trench and set up two posts. They were unable to progress further. By this action and the successes of the right flank of the 7th Division, the left flank of the Australian sector was, henceforth secure.

As already explained, the British 7th Division continued its efforts to capture Bullecourt until relieved on 16 May. On the Australian front, the 2nd Brigade relieved the 1st Brigade on the night of 7 May and the following day launched a diversionary attack along O.G.2 in support of the 7th Division. But, by now, all the units of the 1st Division were exhausted and were progressively relieved by units of the 5th Division. On the morning of 10 May, Brigadier-General J.J.T. Hobbs formally took over responsibility from Major-General N. Smyth.

The first action of the new division was another attempt to reach the point where O.G.2 reached the cross-roads. It was carried out, on 12 May, by the 58th Battalion in support of a further attempt to capture Bullecourt by the 7th Division **(See map 26)**. In order to secure the cross-roads it was necessary to knock out three major German obstacles: a large dugout in Diagonal Road, a machine gun post between O.G.1 and O.G.2 and a post west of the junction. The assault on the dugout was made by three platoons led by Lieutenant F.C.

Letter from the Chaplain of Australian 57th Battalion. Private King's body was not recovered and his name appears on the Villers-Bretonneux Memorial.

Dear Mrs King.

It is with very great sorrow that I am writing to tell you of the death, in action, of your dear son 2675 Pr. King on May 13th near Bullecourt. His battalion was holding the line under very heavy shell fire from the enemy and together with his comrades did splendid work. His body was buried just behind the line & when possible a fitting cross will be erected to his memory. I am painfully aware how little we can comfort you but in your grief you must feel deep pride in the son who gave his life to protect and rescue helpless women and innocent children. You may be assured that his memory will always be revered by the French people and his resting place card for and respected by those whom he died to save.　　　With my sincerest sympathy.

Etc. etc.

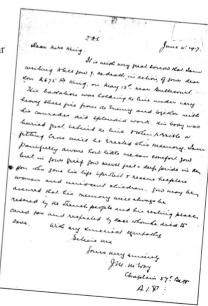

Dawson, whilst a single platoon under Lieutenant R.V. Moon dealt with the machine gun. Both parties were soon held up by a determined German defence, but to their left a platoon under Lieutenant S.J. Topp veered off course and linked up with that of Moon. Topp was almost immediately killed, but the two platoons led by Moon, dealt with the machine gun before moving on to assist with the capture of the dugout. In the course of this, Moon directed a Lewis gun team to jump into a shell-hole from which they could enfilade the area. What followed is described by Bean:

'A minute or two later the Germans broke back to the Diagonal Road. Moon followed, emerged alone into the cutting, and emptied his rifle into them. He was bombed back into the trench. ....After directing a shower of grenades into the cutting, Moon and the nearest Victorians again burst into it. The foremost Germans had been shot down, and it was found that the survivors had, for the moment, withdrawn for shelter into the dugout entrances. Before they could emerge, Moon and his men, firing into the entrances, had them trapped, and kept them there while the rest of the attacking party - now more than thirty strong - was brought up by Dawson, who till then had been pushing forward bombs and reinforcements. Moon began to consolidate in the cutting, while Dawson, taking charge of the 'mopping up', extracted from the dugouts no less than 186 Germans including two officers. .[11]*

For his actions that day Lieutenant Moon was awarded the Victoria Cross.

The cross-roads were not reached due, in part, to heavy rifle and machine gun fire along the road which forced the Australians to withdraw. They returned under cover of darkness to take the position. On the left the Australians reached the road-bank west of the cross-roads and made contact with the 2/Queen's. This left only the south-west corner of the village in enemy hands. However, success was not achieved without losses. In all, the brigade lost 16 officers and over 350 men, but with its task complete, it was withdrawn from the line on the night of 12/13 May to be replaced by the 173rd Brigade of the British 58th (London) Division. Within three days the 58th Division had relieved the 7th Division and took control of the Bullecourt front, leaving the Australians responsible for the ground to the right of Central Road.

By 15 May the Germans were ready to make their seventh, and last, general counter-attack to secure their position at Bullecourt **(See map**

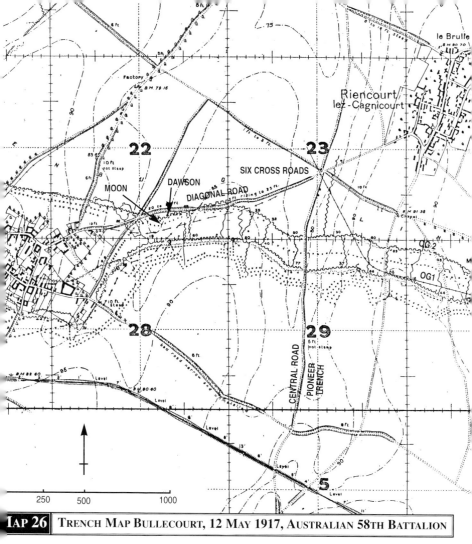

27). At 1.00 a.m. on that day a bombardment commenced falling, initially on the Australian sector, but, by 3.00 a.m., covering the whole of the Bullecourt-Riencourt front. In response, the Australian batteries in Noreuil valley opened up and a dramatic artillery duel ensued. At 3.40 a.m. the German barrage moved forward and the enemy embarked on an attack along the whole front. Troops coming from the direction of Riencourt were cut down, by rifle and machine gun fire, before they reached the front trench O.G.2. Two parties moving westwards, from points in cross-trench "E", managed to enter O.G.2 at its junction with cross-trench "F", before they were ejected.

On the 58th Division front, the 173rd Brigade, Brigadier-General B.C. Freyberg, fought its first battle. Although subjected to the heavy preliminary barrage, the two London battalions, the 2/4 and 2/3, acquitted themselves well. They withstood the initial attack and then drove the enemy back by counter-attacking. So confident were they that the 2/3 was able to send reserves to its right, to back up the Australian 54th Battalion, a gesture which was much appreciated by the battalion commander. Only in Bullecourt did the German attack meet with any success, where the 91st Brigade had to struggle to retain control of the village, to the east of the Longatte road.

It now only remained for the Germans to be expelled from the western part of Bullecourt. Shortly after taking over from Major-General Shoubridge, the commander officer of the 58th Division, Major-General H.D. Fanshawe, set about this task. He had two brigades in the line: the 173rd on the right opposite Riencourt and Hendecourt and the 174th on the left at Bullecourt. The 175th Brigade, having been relieved on the Lagnicourt front by the Australian 8th Brigade, was in reserve. The operation, set for 2.00 a.m. on 17 May, was a frontal assault on the Red Patch by the 2/5 London (London Rifle Brigade), from a line in front of the railway. After a short bombardment, the Londoners swept forward and, meeting little resistance, captured the whole area. When signals were received confirming the success of the 2/5, a company of the 2/8 London (Post Office Rifles) crossed from the Longatte road to clear the rest of the village. Between them they took 36 prisoners. According to the Official History:

> 'The German official communiqué stated that Bullecourt was evacuated in accordance with orders. What actually occurred, as prisoners testified, was that the enemy was caught in the midst of preparations, such as the demolition of cellars and dugouts, for evacuation of the section which he still held.'[12]

Second Bullecourt: The German perspective

When no immediate attack followed the fighting of 11 April, the German headquarters took it to mean that the Australians had suffered to a greater extent than was the case. However, as the Fifth Army prepared to renew the fighting it became clear, from aerial reconnaissance, that further action was not to be long delayed. Accordingly, General Moser set about realigning his forces better to cope with the coming assault. The 27th Division was ordered to hand over the eastern section of its line to the 2nd Guard Reserve Division. This change allowed the regiment so released, the 123rd Grenadier Regiment, to be slotted in between 120th and 124th Infantry

MAP 27 | TRENCH MAP, BULLECOURT, 15 MAY 1917, GERMAN COUNTER-ATTACK

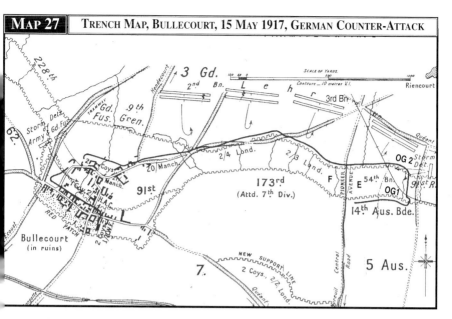

Regiments **(See map 28)**. By the time that General Gough was ready to attack, the Germans were fully prepared. They were also aware of the date of the attack: deduced from the results of further aerial reconnaissance and changes in the pattern of artillery activity. So

Two German soldiers in an advance trench armed with hand grenades. A grenade could be thrown about 50 yards, and the effect of the explosion spread for about 30 yards round, so a mis-throw might have unpleasant effects on the thrower.

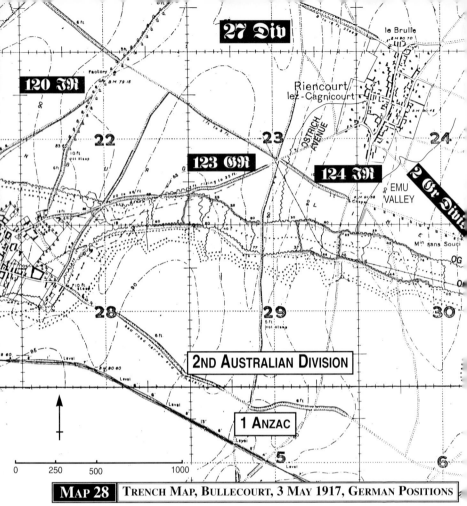

MAP 28 | TRENCH MAP, BULLECOURT, 3 MAY 1917, GERMAN POSITIONS

confident was the commander of the 27th Division in the quality of his intelligence that he ordered an artillery barrage on the area of ground in front of the Australian lines, for 3.30 a.m. on the morning of 3 May.

On the British 62nd Division front, to the west of Bullecourt, it was the 120th IR which quickly restored the line attacked by the 186th and 187th Brigades. To the east of the village, similar results were obtained by the 123rd G.R. with respect to the 185th Brigade. General Moser makes only a passing reference to the presence of tanks with the division and that only on the section defended by the 123 G. R:

> 'Once again the English had in vain put their hopes in the tanks but, stripped of the protection which they expected, their infantry came upon fresh troops on the outskirts of Bullecourt who were prepared to hold on to this important strong point and fight to the last man.'[13]

116

Further to the east the 123 G.R. was less successful where it was up against the left flank of the Australian 6th Brigade. The same is true of the right wing of the 124 I.R., which was attacked by the right flank of the same brigade. The three companies concerned were thrown back and it was here that the Australians gained entry into O.G.1 and O.G.2. The remaining companies of the 124 I.R. were those which successfully withstood the Australian 5th Brigade attack.

General Moser immediately set about rectifying the situation. Reserves were brought up, a counter-attack organised and launched at 8.20 a.m., although Australian records put it somewhat later, at 9.00 a.m. In the course of the Second Battle of Bullecourt the Germans initiated seven such concerted or general, counter-attacks. Each of these will be briefly considered.

Counter-attack No. 1

In this attack the 123rd G.R. bombed up the Hindenburg Line from the west whilst the 124th I.R. attacked from the east. At the same time, a specialist unit of 'Storm Troops' from the 27th Division moved down Ostrich Avenue. They were confident that, by attacking with light 'egg-bombs', which could be thrown much further than the more deadly Mills bomb, they could isolate and overcome the enemy in O.G.1 and O.G.2. But, as noted previously, the Australian commanders had insisted that all the leading troops carried sufficient arms to withstand such tactics. This being the case the counter-attacks were beaten off, and the gains held, although casualty figures were high.

Counter-attack No. 2

This took place at noon, having been ordered at 9.00 a.m., following the earlier failure. The attack was directed towards the same end; driving the Australians out of the two O.G. Lines. The units involved were again the 123rd G.R. and 124th I.R. which attacked in the same locations as earlier. However, on this occasion, the 123rd also provided the troops who worked down Ostrich Avenue leaving the Storm Troops free to carry out a frontal attack.

Counter-attack No. 3

It was this attack which disrupted the modified plan, agreed by Gellibrand and Smyth, for the actions in support of the British 7th Division's attempt to capture Bullecourt. It was directed mainly against the right flank in the Hindenburg Line. In O.G.1, the 28th Battalion was driven out for the third time but with the help of two trench-mortars, managed to regain their positions in both lines. Again,

German records show that, it was the 124th I.R. which was involved. On the other flank, the 123rd G.R. attacked somewhat later but was repulsed.

Counter-attack No. 4

This was the counter-attack which the Australian 6th Brigade helped to repel as it was being relieved. It had been timed for dawn in the vicinity of Central Road and was carried out by part of the 120th I.R. from divisional reserve. In the west, the 123rd G.R. was again used. Both attacks were assisted by *Flammenwerfer.*

Counter-attack No. 5

By the evening of 4 May General Moser had brought up three fresh infantry battalions to support his over-stretched 27th Division. Again attacks were launched on both sides of the Australian line: in the east, the 2nd Battalion of the 98 Reserve Infantry Regiment R.I.R. led a flank attack supported by the 3rd Battalion of the same regiment. In the west, the 2nd Battalion Lehr (Training) 3rd Guard Regiment attacked, assisted by the 123rd G.R. on the flank. Only on the Australian 3rd Battalion front were any gains made.

Counter-attack No. 6

Before this attack was carried out, further changes in personnel had taken place on the German side. The 1st Battalion of the 98th R.I.R. replaced the 123rd G.R. All units in the east, by now very mixed, were withdrawn and replaced by the 1st Battalion of the Lehr Regiment. The attack was sent in at dawn on 6 May and once again *Flammenwerfer* played an important part. It failed to make ground in O.G. 1 but did so in O.G.2 but was eventually driven back. It was in this attack that Corporal Howell won the Victoria Cross.

Counter-attack No. 7

The final counter-attack took place on the night of 14/15 May at 1.00 a.m. The reason for the long delay between the sixth and seventh attacks was that the German commanders were not satisfied with earlier bombardments. They felt that herein lay the reason for the failures. Accordingly, a longer, more intense, bombardment was ordered. At the same time, supplies of shells were delayed and the attack originally scheduled for 9 May was put back to 15 May. On the evening of 14 May, the 2nd and 3rd Battalions of the Lehr Regiment took their positions **(See map 27)**. That the result was another failure contributed to the ending of the Second Battle of Bullecourt.

Conclusions

In the two battles of Bullecourt the British suffered in excess of 14,000 casualties. I Anzac Corps lost approximately 300 officers and 7,000 other ranks and similar total figures were recorded by the other units of V Corps. In the period immediately following the war these casualty figures were deemed to be jointly the responsibility of General Gough and the Commander-in Chief, Sir Douglas Haig. Gough was condemned on three counts: for his insistence on attacking at a re-entrant, ignoring the fire power of the Germans in Quéant and even though the line of attack failed in April, for attacking in the same place in May. Haig was criticised for his insistence, in the second battle, that all units involved on the Arras front attack at the same time, thereby depriving the Australians of the cover of darkness, to avoid the well-positioned German machine guns. In addition, Haig's decision to prolong the fighting for Bullecourt was also questioned. Such criticism was probably unfair given the necessity to render the Australian position secure and the need to aid the French.

More recently the actions of the Australian staff, particularly in the preparation for, and the execution of, the first day of the second battle have been re-assessed. The failure of the 5th Brigade is now considered to be, at least in part, the fault of Brigadier-General Smith and the I Anzac staff. Smith, like Gough, failed to take account of the machine guns in, and around, Quéant. These should have been destroyed as part of the preliminary artillery barrage. Instead the barrage concentrated

The railway embankment near Bullecourt, used during the attacks on the Hindenburg Line as battalion or brigade headquarters, after the Australians had moved forward.

Australian troops, in a sunken section of road near Noreuil, in May 1917 after the capture of Bullecourt.

on the German supply lines. Smith is also criticised for his choice of headquarters, in Noreuil, too far behind his brigade. In this he is contrasted with Gellibrand who had his headquarters in the railway embankment.

Epilogue

After Bullecourt had been captured units of the British 58th Division found themselves detailed to clear up what remained of the village. In the History of the Post Office Rifles, Charles Messenger quotes the following unattributed experience:

> *'By this time Bullecourt and its surroundings had become a veritable charnel house; dead bodies and dead mules lying around in hundreds, and the place so offensive that it was a question whether it could be retained. Parties were organised to clear up, and in a short space of time, in spite of every adverse*

condition, it was made tolerably healthy. An amusing incident occurred in connection with five dead mules, which had become particularly offensive and defied removal. A party of twenty volunteers (B Company) under an officer were chosen and given carte blanche as to methods; their report, which was forwarded to Brigade, is as follows: "the five dead mules are no longer offensive. The site of their grave is marked by an empty rum-jar, the contents of which assisted in the operation".' [14]*

ALL BULLECOURT BRITISH.

WON AFTER 15 DAYS' FIGHTING.

STUBBORNLY DEFENDED VILLAGE.

The following telegraphic dispatches were re-ived from General Headquarters in France
sterday : —

1.48 A.M.—Fighting again took place during the night in Bullecourt. Our troops have made further progress through e village and have reached its western edge.

8.42 P.M.—To-day, our troops completed the pture of Bullecourt, taking some 60 prisoners. The whole of the village, for the possession of hich constant fighting has taken place since the d inst., is now in our hands.

. It was on May 3, when the Battle of Arras flared again after an interval of comparative quiet, that llecourt, which is in the Hindenburg line, was acked. Australian troops, moving out from below llecourt, breached the Hindenburg line well, to the st of the village, and, in spite of almost daily unter-attacks, have since then not only maintained, t extended, their gains. English troops broke into village, but they were unable to hold all the ound won owing to the severe machine-gun fire ought to bear on them. Now, after a fortnight's hting, in which attack and counter-attack have ernated, the whole of the village has passed into r possession.

"2.300 ENGLISH PRISONERS" IN MAY.

GERMAN official reports, May 17 :—
FRONT OF CROWN PRINCE RUPPRECHT.—As a con-
quei   e had

Bibliography

1 *The Official History of Australia in the War 1914-1918.* Volume IV. Bean. 1933.
2 Ibid.
3 *War Diary 1st Tank Corps HQ.* Public Record Office. WO 95/97.
4 *The History of the 62nd (West Riding) Division 1914-1919.* Everard Wyrall. John Lane.
5 Ibid.
6 *The Official History of Australia in the War 1914-1918.* Volume IV. Bean. 1933.
7 Ibid.
8 *The Seventh Division 1914-1918.* C.T. Atkinson. John Murray. London. 1927.
9 Ibid.
10 Ibid.
11 *The Official History of Australia in the War 1914-1918.* Volume IV. Bean. 1933.
12 *Military Operations in France & Belgium.* 1917 Volume I. Falls. Macmillan 1940.
13 *Die Württemberger im Weltkrieg.* Otto von Moser.
14 *Terriers in the Trenches. The History of the Post Office Rifles.* Messenger. Picton Publishing. 1982.

Bullecourt Captured.

The Times, Friday 18 May 1917.

Chapter Five

MAJOR PERCY BLACK AND PRINCE
FRIEDRICH OF PRUSSIA

Major Percy Charles Herbert Black DSO, DCM. (1879-1917)

At 4.45 a.m. on 11 April 1917, the 16th Battalion AIF climbed out of their line in the sunken road in front of the Hindenburg Line and advanced. On the right of the battalion front was "B" Company under Major P.C.H. Black DSO, DCM. Half-way to the objective two of their three tanks had stopped, but the battalion pushed on although under very heavy fire. They reached their first objective, but in greatly reduced numbers, both from machine gun fire and from the bomb fight which ensued after they passed through the first belt of wire. As they tried to move on to the second objective they ran into uncut wire. Black led his men along the wire, searching for a break, but in so doing he was shot in the head and killed. His great friend, Captain (later Lieutenant-Colonel) H. Murray VC, reported seeing Black's body hanging on the wire. After the fighting died down Murray searched for the body but without success. Major Black is commemorated at Villers-Bretonneux.

Percy Charles Herbert Black was born on 12 December 1879 at Beremboke, Gelong, Victoria, the eleventh child of Irish parents. He started his working life as a carpenter but tiring of this, moved to Western Australia and became a gold prospector. When war broke out, still in Western Australia, he joined the AIF. He went to Gallipoli with the 16th Battalion where he served in one of the battalion machine gun teams. On 25 April the battalion, under Lieutenant-Colonel H. Pope, landed during the day and pushed on up to the head of Monash Valley and occupied a wedge-shaped hill, afterwards known as Pope's Hill. On the following morning, the Turks began to creep across the head of Monash Valley to a position from which they were able to snipe at the Australians on Pope's Hill. The main body of troops were in trenches but the supports, on the rear of the hill, had little or no protection. The two battalion machine guns were positioned to deal with the Turks and the leader of one of the gun crews was Percy Black. Alongside him was Private Harry Murray, who, as mentioned above, finished the war as a Lieutenant-Colonel. The two machine gunners fought until both guns were smashed by Turkish bullets. Percy Black was first wounded in the arm and later shot through the ear.

On 8 August Black was involved in the fighting around Hill 971. Shrapnel from the hill was falling over the spur on which the 16th Battalion was positioned. As the Turks came forward it seemed that the position would be overrun until Black, now promoted Lieutenant, along with Lieutenant Blainey and Sergeant Murrray, set up their machine guns and ensured the safety of the brigade's retreat. For his exploits at Gallipoli Black was awarded the DCM. By 1916 Black had risen to the rank of major, when he took part in the fighting at Pozières and Mouquet Farm. Two further awards followed: the DSO and the Croix de Guerre.

Bean relates that, unbeknown to Black, his admirers openly referred to him as 'the bravest in the AIF'. Writing in the Journal of the Australian War Memorial, Elizabeth Burness quotes from a reminiscence written, by his old friend, Lieutenant-Colonel H. Murray, in 1936.

> '... many think that Black did not fear death but one or two of us who were his intimate friends knew he had all the natural fear of the unknown, but that never did he let it influence his actions when in danger. He had the superstitions of the highlander ... a day or two before Bullecourt, speaking to him for a few minutes he said quite calmly, "Harry this will be my last fight, but I'll have that bloody German trench before they get me". Percy seldom used an oath - so I knew he was in deadly earnest.'[1]

On 23 April 1988 a painting, by the Australian war artist James Scott, was given to the village of Bullecourt by the Australian War Memorial. It depicts the death of Major Percy Black and now hangs in the Mairie in Bullecourt. The picture was presented to the inhabitants of the village in recognition of the way in which, for over 70 years, they had remembered the Australians who fought in the two battles of Bullecourt in 1917 a remembrance very much carried on today.

Prince Friedrich Karl of Prussia (1891-1917)

On the afternoon of Wednesday 21 March 1917, men of the Australian 26th Battalion, in trenches in front of Vaulx Wood (Bois de Vaulx), were amazed to see an enemy aircraft forced to land in No Man's Land, 200 yards in front of their position. The pilot climbed out of the cockpit and ran towards the German lines. As he did so, the Australians opened fire and brought him down. Several Australians then went forward and brought the pilot back. He was found to be badly wounded but was able to tell them that he was Prince Friedrich Karl of Prussia. He was taken to an aid post but died later in hospital. The aircraft was also recovered and hidden behind a small copse.

Prince Friedrich Karl was the great grand-nephew of Kaiser Wilhelm I and a second cousin of Kaiser Wilhelm II. His great grandfather, Prince Karl, was a brother of Wilhelm I. He was the second son of Prince Friedrich Leopold and was also a nephew of the Duke of Connaught. He was born in 1891 and in April 1916 married Princess Marie of Schaumberg-Lippe. The Prince was an accomplished tennis player. A few years before the war he entered the Wimbledon Lawn Tennis Championships under the name 'F. Karl'. It took the authorities and other players some time to identify him but many thought, wrongly, that he was the Prussian Crown Prince.

He was also an enthusiastic airman but due to his rank was not permitted to join a combat squadron. On the afternoon in question he had obtained permission to fly with the commander of a fighting formation. He was supplied with an aircraft which carried not only the distinctive German cross but, also, a skull and cross bones The patrol was met by No. 32 Squadron RFC and in the ensuing dog-fight the Prince's plane was forced down. The British pilot, Lieutenant C.E.M. Pickthorne, having established that the troops surrounding the German pilot were British, landed. He was then informed of the pilot's name and rank. The following day, Pickhorne returned to the Australian lines with the intention of flying back the captured enemy aircraft. Unfortunately the petrol tank was found to be holed, so the plane had to be brought back by road. It was later put on display in Bapaume.

Early on Friday 23 March a British aircraft dropped the following message over German lines:

To German Royal Flying Corps.

Prince Frederick Charles was brought down on 21.3.17 and is now in hospital seriously wounded.

Lagnicourt Valley where the plane of Prince Friedrich of Prussian was forced down by Lieutenant Pickthorne.

We should be very grateful if you could give us any information of:

2/Lt. M.J. Mare-Montembault	*missing 6.3.17.*
2/Lt. E.G. Wagner	*missing 7.1.17.*
2/Lt. H. Blythe	*missing 2.2.17.*
Lt. H.G. Southon	*missing 6.3.17.*

A reply from the Germans was dropped over British lines and relayed to the squadron by the Australian 2nd Division at 5.30 p.m. In the message the Germans requested further details of the Prince's condition. No mention was made of the four British airmen.

Both Second Lieutenant Wagner and Second Lieutenant Blythe died on the days on which they were reported missing. Second Lieutenant Wagner is

---

Wednesday 21st March 1917

Lt. Billinge is appointed Acting Flight Commander 11.3.17. vice Capt. J.U. Robb.

Lt J.A. Aronson is posted from 29th to this Squadron 19.3.17.

Lt. T.A. Cooch was discharged Hospital 19.3.17.

One line patrol only carried out during which Lt. Pickthorne drove one hostile machine down. The patrol met 6 Halburstadts and a combat ensued at very close quarters, during which Lt. Pickthorne got on ones tail. He fired one double drum into it driving it down until it landed under control. Lt. Pickthorne having ascertained that the troops were British landed and found it intact, and that the pilot, who was found to be Prince Frederick Charles, had been taken away wounded.

A party was at once sent out to recover the hostile machine.

Extract from No. 32 Squadron Diary November 1916 - November 1917. PRO Air 1/1494/204/38/4.

Prince Friedrich Karl of Prussia's plane on display in Bapaume, 22 March 1917. IWM Q36249

buried in Achiet-Le-Grand Communal Cemetery Extension and Second Lieutenant Blythe in Croisilles British Cemetery. Second Lieutenant Mare-Montembault and Lieutenant Southon were prisoners of war.

Bibliography

1. *Journal of the Australian War Memorial.* No. 15 October 1989.

Chapter Six

FIVE VICTORIA CROSSES

The Victoria Cross was founded by Royal Warrant on 29 January 1856. Originally awarded to men of the army and navy, the warrant has been amended several times and now allows for the award to be made to other categories of recipient. The Maltese Cross is still made of bronze from cannon captured during the Crimean War and carries the inscription 'For Valour'. During April and May 1917 five Victoria Crosses were awarded for deeds in and near Bullecourt.

Captain James Ernest Newland 12th Australian Infantry Battalion A.I.F.

By early April 1917, there were but three villages between the southern division of I Anzac and the Hindenburg Line: Boursies, Demicourt and Hermies **(See map 15)**. Hermies was considered to be the most difficult to take and was allocated to the 1st Brigade. The capture of Boursies, lying either side of the Bapaume - Cambrai road, was to undertaken by the 12th Battalion 3rd Brigade. Anzac staff considered that the easiest way to capture Hermies would be to strike ostensibly at Boursies, and under cover of this 'diversion' to attack Hermies. With these villages in Australian hands it was predicted that the Germans would evacuate Demicourt.

At 3.00 a.m. on Sunday 8 April, a platoon of B Company 12th Battalion, led by Lieutenant Newitt, moved to the right of the main road and to a position about J.10.b.1.4 to 1.9 **(See map 29)**. At about the same time, A Company under Captain Newland moved forward, under cover of the bank in J.4.central, before wheeling right to attack the mill at J.5.c.2.0. Aided by a diversion created by Lieutenant Newitt, Newland's men made good progress across the open (a distance of about 300 yards) before a heavy machine gun opened fire, causing heavy casualties. Newland pushed the attack home, himself leading a bombing party, which led the enemy to abandon the strong position. Two Germans, in advance bomb posts, were bayoneted. A party of 6 Germans, near the road in J.5.c.central, surrendered and then threw a percussion bomb. They were immediately killed as a reward for their treachery! Captain Newland then proceeded to set up a Lewis machine gun post beyond the mill, guarding the main road, along with two further posts in J.5.c. At dawn B Company's platoons occupied the trench in J.10.b. without opposition.

A Company at the mill were heavily shelled all the following day. At about 2.00 p.m., under cover of a blizzard, a party of Germans rushed the mill from the main road but were driven off through the prompt action of Sergeant L.G. Scott, who shot four men in succession. At 10.00 p.m., a further counter-attack was launched, under the cover of a heavy bombardment by pineapple trench mortars and smoke bombs, from the trenches in J.5.a. and J.5.c. Bombs were also thrown from the road and Newland's two posts, near the road, were forced to fall back until reorganised by Sergeant Whittle and Captain Newland. With the help of a platoon of D Company the counter-attack was driven back.

The 12th Battalion remained in position until relieved by the 11th Battalion on 10 April. The battalion returned to the line on the evening of 14 April at Lagnicourt. The night was quiet, but an hour before dawn the enemy struck. All four companies were attacked and Newland's A Company soon found themselves fighting on three sides. He therefore fell back to the sunken Lagnicourt - Doignies road where he managed to halt the breakthrough **(See map 16)**. It was in the course of this

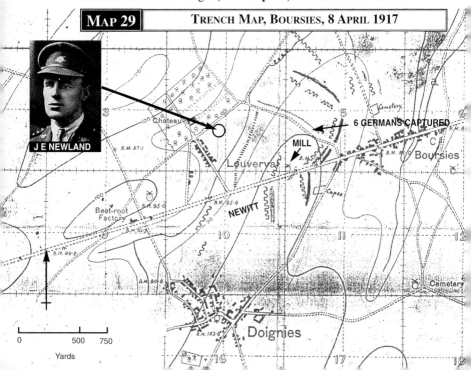

MAP 29 TRENCH MAP, BOURSIES, 8 APRIL 1917

J E NEWLAND

6 GERMANS CAPTURED

MILL

Boursies

Louverval

NEWITT

Château

Beet-root Factory

Doignies

Cemetery

0   500   750

Yards

action that Sergeant Whittle knocked out a machine gun.

The citation for the Victoria Cross, awarded to Newland, referred to conspicuous bravery on three occasions: at Boursies, the capture of the mill and the defeat of the night counter-attack, and at Lagnicourt.

James Newland was born at Highton, Gelong Victoria on 22 August 1881. At the time of the award of the Victoria Cross he was almost thirty-six years old. He was, therefore, the oldest member of the AIF to be so decorated. He enlisted at the age of 18 and served in South Africa. After a period of five years with the artillery he was appointed to the Instructional Staff of the Commonwealth Military Forces. He transferred to the AIF in August 1914, joining the 12th Battalion as Regimental Quarter Master Sergeant.

He served in Gallipoli, where he was wounded for the first time. He was commissioned Second Lieutenant in May 1915 and promoted to Lieutenant in October of the same year. After the evacuation he went to Egypt before arriving in France, in time to take part in the fighting at Pozières in July and August 1916. Following the German retreat to the Hindenburg Line he was twice more wounded, in late February and in May.

He returned to Australia in 1918 and served as an officer in the Permanent Forces, holding various appointments, until he retired with the honorary rank of lieutenant-colonel in August 1941. He died in Caulfield, Victoria in March 1948.

Sergeant John Woods Whittle 12th Australian Infantry Battalion A.I.F.

The story of Sergeant Whittle is almost the story of Captain Newland. Both were members of the 12th Battalion and both were involved in the deeds for which Whittle was decorated. When A Company moved on the mill at the start of the attack at Boursies it did so, in two waves, on a four platoon front. The platoon on the right was led by Lieutenant A.A. Heritage, the two in the centre by Lieutenant W.J. Kelly and Lieutenant R. Sherwin and that on the left by Sergeant Whittle. After the mill had been captured Captain Newland ordered Sergeant Whittle to take command of one of the posts set up between the mill and the village. Following the German counter-attack at 10 p.m. the next day Whittle showed extraordinary courage and resolution in collecting and re-organising the remaining men, before leading an attack on the enemy.

On 15 April, when the Germans attacked at Lagnicourt, Whittle was again serving with Captain Newland. When the enemy attacked, and broke through, they organised a defensive line along the banks of the sunken road running from Lagnicourt - Doignies **(See map 16)**. As they fought to hold the line Whittle saw a group of Germans in the process of setting up a machine gun, near an oratory on the edge of the village. Without hesitation he set off, across open ground, to destroy the gun before it could be brought into operation. Having knocked out the post, he took charge of the machine gun, and returned to the Australian line. If the gun had been allowed to open fire it would have decimated the troops in the sunken road, allowing the German attack to progress. In the subsequent Australian counter-attack all the lost ground was recovered. Whittle was awarded the Victoria Cross for his actions at Boursies and Lagnicourt.

John Whittle was born on 3 August 1883 at Huon Island, in the Port Cygnet district of Tasmania. Like Newland, he saw service with the Australian contingent in South Africa, before joining the Royal Navy, as a stoker. After five years he returned to the army serving successively in the Army Service Corps, the Artillery and the Tasmanian Rifle Regiment. In August 1915 he joined the AIF and, on arrival in Egypt, was assigned to the 12th Battalion. The battalion moved to France, in the Spring of 1916, where he was wounded in June.

In 1917 he was awarded the DCM in the battalion's actions at Le Barque and Ligny-Thilloy. He was wounded a second time, in the German assault in March 1918, and again in late July. He returned to Australia, where he was involved in recruitment, until the war ended. After leaving the army in December 1918 he moved to Sydney, where he died on 2 March 1946.

Lieutenant Charles Pope 11th Australian Infantry Battalion A.I.F.

The award to Lieutenant Pope also resulted from the German attack in the vicinity of Lagnicourt on 15 April 1917. The citation stated that the award was made for 'conspicuous bravery and devotion to duty when in command of a very important picquet'. When the Germans broke through the picquet was surrounded, and out of ammunition, Pope led the picquet in a charge to stem the attack. The citation continues, 'By his sacrifice, Lieutenant Pope not only inflicted heavy loss on the enemy, but obeyed his order to

hold the position to the last'.

The line occupied by the 11th Battalion was not the conventional, heavily defended line, but consisted of a series of widely separated picquets. The portion held by the A Company ran from D.30.a.4.6 to D.30.c1.4.(See map 30). This was the right sector of the line which continued as indicated on the map. At about 4.00 a.m. an intense enemy artillery barrage was directed on the picquet line and on the ground behind as far back as Louverval. After about 15 minutes, A Company reported that the enemy had broken through C Company on its left, and was advancing on them from the direction of D.22.d. The battalion commander, Major R.A. Rafferty, sent forward another half company from his reserve, in the sunken road through D.28.c, to assist A Company. As the reserves moved up the right flank of A Company was forced to fall back, in concert with the 4th Battalion on its right, to a position in D.28.d. But by this time the centre picquet was surrounded and had used up all its ammunition. With fixed bayonets the remainder of the post, lead by Lieutenant Pope, charged into a large body of the enemy during which attack - or soon after - Pope was killed. The left picquet of A Company, under the command of Lieutenant P.W. Lyon, held out, after the company on its left had been broken, thereby gaining time for his company commander to make good his rear line of resistance. This action lead to the loss of Lieutenant Lyon and his platoon. A Company eventually established a line approximately D.29.d.5.0 to D.29.a.0.0. The exact position of Pope's charge is not clear, even in the report in the battalion war diary, but must have been somewhere in the area indicated on map 30.

After the enemy withdrawal Pope's body was recovered. Nearby were about eighty dead Germans. Lieutenant Pope is buried in

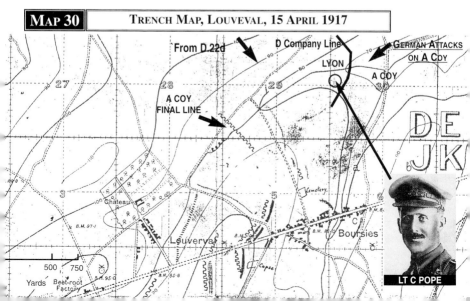

MAP 30 — **TRENCH MAP, LOUVEVAL, 15 APRIL 1917**

Mœuvres Communal Cemetery Extension, V.D.22.

Charles Pope was born at Mile End, London, on 5 March 1883. He went to Canada and worked on the railways, before returning to London in 1900 to join the Metropolitan Police. He remained in the police until 1909 when he again decided to move abroad, this time to Australia. He enlisted in the AIF in August 1915, was commissioned Second Lieutenant in February 1916 and promoted to Lieutenant in December 1916.

Corporal George Julian Howell. 1st Australian Infantry Battalion A.I.F.

The Germans launched their sixth general counter-attack during the Second Battle of Bullecourt, at dawn on 6 May. The 1st Battalion, 3rd Brigade was in O.G.1 to the left of Central Road **(See map 33)**. This battalion was not at first involved but, at about 6.00 a.m., Corporal G.J. Howell, commanding a post near Central Road sent a message back to the battalion headquarters stating that 'the battalion on the right is retiring'. The battalion commander, Captain A. K. Mackenzie, hurriedly mustered all available men in and near the headquarters, to resist the enemy onslaught. Led by the battalion signalling officer they moved to the edge of Central Road and, under a deluge of egg and stick bombs, commenced to throw grenades in return. Two German officers, leading the attack, were killed and as the Australians prepared to move down O.G.1 Corporal Howell was seen to scramble out on to the open parapet of the trench and run along it throwing bombs on to the Germans. They quickly retreated, pursued by Howell, until he was hit and fell into the trench badly wounded. Shortly after, the counter-attack faltered and, all the lost ground was recovered.

George Howell known as 'Snowy' was born in Sydney on 23 November 1893. On leaving school he took up bricklaying and then worked as a builder. On enlistment he was posted to the 1st Battalion, in Gallipoli, in November 1915. In 1916 he arrived in France and was wounded at Pozières in July. In February 1917 he was promoted to corporal and in April awarded the MM for his work at Demicourt. However, the wounds he received at Bullecourt were so severe that his war was over. After a long period in hospital he was returned to Australia and discharged in June 1918.

Between the wars he worked in newspaper advertising but was

accepted back into the army with the onset of hostilities in 1939. He served as a staff sergeant before joining the United States Sea Transport Service in August 1944. In this unit he took part in the invasion of Leyte at the start of the Philippines campaign. He died on 23 December 1964.

Lieutenant Rupert Vance Moon. 58th Australian Infantry Battalion A.I.F.

The second Battle of Bullecourt was nearing its end when Lieutenant Rupert Moon won the Victoria Cross. He was initially considered, by Brigadier-General H.E. Elliot, to be too diffident to be a successful commander of men!

Yet he produced a magnificent display of persistence and determination when detailed to assist the British 7th Division on 12 May. The 58th Battalion attacked three centres of German opposition: a large dugout, a concrete machine gun post and another post beyond the first two.

In the fighting for the concrete machine gun post Moon was wounded in the face but he went on to help with the capture of the dugout. Leaving a 'mopping up' party to deal with the dugout, Moon decided to get his men dug in, in a safer position, nearer to his own lines. Before moving he looked over the parapet to locate the enemy and was hit in the face. His jaw was broken and the flesh mutilated. Nevertheless he insisted on seeing the men into the new position before allowing himself to be taken to the rear. In all Moon was wounded four times.

Rupert Moon was born on 14 August 1892 at Bacchus Marsh, Victoria. After school he followed his father into banking. He had pre-war military experience in Light Horse and infantry regiments but when he enlisted in September 1914 he expressed a preference for the Light Horse. He served with the 4th Light Horse Regiment in Gallipoli, where the regiment was used as infantry. By March 1916 he had reached the rank of sergeant. He was commissioned Second Lieutenant in September of the same year and posted to the 58th Battalion. When he recovered from his Bullecourt wounds he was decorated by King George V, in London, in August 1917. He left the army in October 1919 with the honorary rank of captain.

He returned to banking, for a short period, before becoming an accountant, a profession which, he followed for many years. He died in Melbourne on 28 February 1986.

Chapter Seven

BATTLEFIELD TOURS

Introduction

The sites of all the actions described in this book can, unusually, be found on one map. Bullecourt village is quite small and most of the principal sites are easily reached on foot. However, to cover the fighting at Lagnicourt is more difficult and best carried out by car or bicycle. In common with most battlefields the ground is fairly open with little or no cover. Therefore, if walking the ground, come equipped with clothing suitable for all weathers. In particular make sure you have a hat to combat the cold winds in winter and the sun in

C.W.G.C. map of cemeteries in the area around Bullecourt.

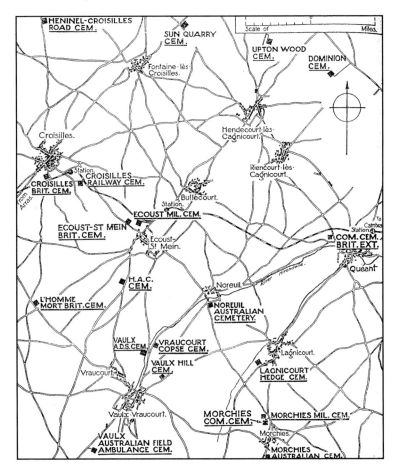

summer. Heavy shoes or, better still, boots are advisable as the ground can be rough, wet and muddy. Always carry a supply of liquid, either hot or cold, and some food, if only a bar of chocolate.

All the tours in this section start from, or close to, Bullecourt village. Reaching Bullecourt is covered in the earlier section, Advice to Travellers. If you are intending to follow the walks you will need to park your car and suitable places have been suggested. Make sure you do not leave your vehicle where it can cause obstruction, especially to agricultural vehicles. In addition, do not leave valuables on view. Put them out of sight, in the boot, to avoid temptation.

It is recommended that a tour around the battlefield by car is carried out before attempting any of the walks. This will give an overall view and indeed, for many people, may be sufficient to get a feel for the fighting. For this reason, visits to cemeteries and the sites of major memorials have been included in the general tour, although fuller details of the latter are included in the walks. In addition to the maps in this book you will need the IGN (Institut Gèographique National) Blue Series 1: 25 000. This may be bought in England at good booksellers or by members of the Western Front Association from the marketing officer. Maps in the series are often available at French supermarkets or in 'Maison de la Presse' shops such as the one in the centre of Bapaume. The map required is 2507 O (Croisilles).

A General Tour of the Bullecourt and Lagnicourt Battlefields

Maps: *IGN Blue Series 2507 O Croisilles.*   **Maps 31 and 8, 16, 30, 25.**

Cemeteries included in the tour:
Quéant Communal Cemetery Extension, Vaulx Hill, Quéant Road, Buissy, Vraucourt Copse British, Lagnicourt Hedge, Ecoust British, Louverval Military

Enter Bullecourt on the D 956 and follow the road to pass, on the right, the 'slouch hat' memorial, and on the left, the Mairie and the village war memorial. Continue on the road and shortly, bear right on to the Rue des Australiens and follow the sign post to the Bullecourt Australian Memorial. This memorial, on the right hand side of the road, is in the form of an Australian 'Digger' and stands in the ground between the two trench lines, O.G.1 and O.G.2, of the Hindenburg Line. Continue along the road, which becomes sunken, until you reach a second memorial on the left hand side of the road. This is known as the Cross Memorial and was erected at the point where trench O.G.2

135

joined the road. The trench then followed the road back past the 'Digger' before turning to pass behind the village. The section of road near the junction with O.G.2 was known as Diagonal Road. It was close to the memorial that Lieutenant Rupert Moon, 58th Battalion AIF, won his Victoria Cross.

Shortly after passing the cross you will reach the Six Cross Roads. There are now only five, as one was not re-established after the war, but this sixth road is shown on the map as in 1917. The track which joins the road from the right is the track known as Central Road, which played a very important role in the Australian attacks. Continue along the road into Riencourt where the road bears right and becomes the D 38. You will pass a water tower on the left before seeing, directly ahead, a small oratory, Notre Dame de la Delivrance. If you stop near the oratory you can see Bullecourt church at 9 o'clock; the road past the

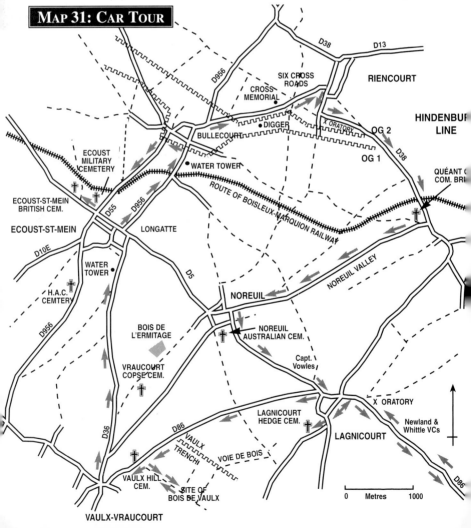

MAP 31: CAR TOUR

Quéant Communal Cemetery British Extension.

oratory eventually becomes the track which ran parallel with Central Road. Return to the D 38 and continue towards Quéant. As the road rises it is crossed by a line of pylons from which point a clear view of the battlefield can be gained. Both trenches of the Hindenburg Line crossed this road as did the two lines of the Drocourt-Quéant Switch **(See map 8).**

Before reaching Quéant you will pass Quéant Communal Cemetery British Extension, on the right hand side of the road. This cemetery was begun during the advance to victory in September 1918. Among the soldiers buried here is Lieutenant Samuel Lewis Honey VC, DCM, MM, 78th Battalion CEF who was

The Oratory, Notre Dame de la Delivrance, Riencourt.

posthumously awarded the Victoria Cross for his actions during the fighting for Bourlon Wood in September and October 1918. Also buried here is Major-General Louis James Lipsett CB, CMG, Royal Irish Regiment, G.O.C. the British 4th Division, who was killed, by machine gun fire whilst reconnoitring in front of Vordon Wood, near Saulzoir on 14 October 1918. He was buried the following day in the presence of H.R.H. the Prince of Wales, the G.O.C. First Army, Sir Arthur Currie (Commander of the Canadian Corps) and other senior officers.

On leaving the cemetery there are alternatives routes. The one shown on map 31 requires that you take the sharp right hand turning at the end of the cemetery. However, you may wish to visit Quéant Road Cemetery, Buissy, which can be reached by continuing into Quéant and taking the D 14 to Buissy. The cemetery is about two and a half kilometres from Quéant, on the left hand side of the road immediately before the junction with the D 14E to Cagnicourt and Inchy-en-Artois. It was made by the 2nd and 57th Casualty Clearing Stations in the last two months of the war. At that time it contained only seventy-one burials but was enlarged, after the Armistice, by the concentration of 2226 graves from other nearby cemeteries. There are now more Australians buried here than in any other cemetery in the area, many

of them unknown. Among the graves are those of Captain P. Cherry VC, MC, Major B Leane and Sergeant J. White.

Captain Percy Cherry, 26th Battalion AIF, was killed in action 27 March 1917. He had established his reputation, during the previous August, at Pozières. He was awarded the Victoria Cross for his work in the fighting for Lagnicourt. The London Gazette 11 May 1917 states that the award was made for 'most conspicuous bravery; determination and leadership in command of a company detailed to storm and clear a village. After all the other officers of his company had become casualties he carried on with care and determination in the face of fierce opposition and cleared the village of the enemy. He sent frequent reports of progress made and, when held up for some time by an enemy strong point, he organised machine gun and bomb parties and captured the position. His leadership, coolness and bravery set a wonderful example to his men. Having cleared the village, he took charge of the situation, and beat off the most resolute and heavy counter-attacks made by the enemy. Wounded about 6.30 a.m., he refused to leave his post, and there remained, encouraging all to hold out at all costs, until about 4.30 p.m., this very gallant officer was killed by an enemy shell'. Captain Cherry is buried to the rear of the cemetery in grave number VIII C.10.

Captain PH Cherry VC. Quéant Road Cemetery, Buissy.

Major B.B. Leane was killed on 10 April 1917, in the withdrawal, following the failure of the morning attack. Sergeant Jack White, 22nd Battalion AIF, was killed on 3 May 1917. However, his body remained undiscovered until a French farmer, ploughing his fields near Bullecourt, disturbed the remains nearly eighty years later. Found at the same time were some of the sergeant's possessions, including a wallet and a lock of hair, believed to have belonged to his wife Lilian. He was finally laid to rest in Quéant Road Cemetery, in October 1995, in the presence of members of his family, and representatives of, the local community, the Australian Embassy (Paris) and the Commonwealth War Graves Commission. The lock of hair remains with him.

Now return to Quéant Communal Cemetery and take the turning on the right, at the end of the cemetery, referred to earlier. Ignore the small

View from Lagnicourt Hedge Cemetery showing the Australian 2nd Brigade artillery positions on 15 April 1917. The site of Captain Vowles' action is also indicated.

turning on the right and bear to the left. You are now entering Noreuil valley which was the site of numerous Australian artillery positions. The road was used to bring prisoners and wounded back from the front line. Eventually Noreuil church appears directly in front of you. On reaching Noreuil, turn left on to the D 5 to Lagnicourt. The road climbs up past the communal cemetery, on the right hand side, before dropping down into Lagnicourt. A large agricultural building, on the left hand side of the road, marks the area where Captain Vowles was located during the fighting on 15 April 1917. Just past the building is the track where the machine gun was positioned **(See map 16)**. As you enter the village the D 5 bears to the left. Continue on this road and bear right over a small bridge. Take the D 18, on the right, to Morchies and Bertincourt and bear right again to visit Lagnicourt Hedge Cemetery. This cemetery was begun by the Somerset Light Infantry in June 1917 and used until November 1917. Plot II was made in March 1918, by the enemy who called the cemetery Lagnicourt Cemetery No. 2, having three others in the commune. Plot I was completed by the Guards Division in September 1918. The cemetery contains 61 UK burials, one Australian and one unknown. From the cemetery a good view can be obtained of the site of Captain Vowles' action and the position of the guns of Australian 2nd Brigade **(See map 16)**. Return to the D 5 and continue in the direction of Doignies and Hermies. The road climbs out of the village and almost at the top of the hill, on the left hand side, is a small oratory. On reaching the crest of the hill the road is sunken on both sides. It was in this section of road that Captain Newland and Sergeant Whittle carried out the second of the actions for which they were both awarded Victoria Crosses.

If you wish it is now possible to visit the site where Lieutenant Pope won his Victoria Cross, but this is not shown on map 31. Continue on the D 5 for about 4 kilometres to reach the N 30 Bapaume to Cambrai road. Turn left on to this road to Boursies. On the left hand side you will pass the Louverval Military Cemetery and Memorial, at Doignies. The cemetery is below the level of the road and even the Cross of Sacrifice is barely visible. The memorial records the names of over seven thousand missing from the Battle of Cambrai November and December 1917. Carry on through Boursies and take the road on the left at the end of the village, to Inchy-en-Artois. Pope was in the ground to your left behind the village **(See map 30)**. Retrace your steps to the site of the action of Newlands and Whittle.

If you have visited Boursies you can continue back into Lagnicourt. If not, a short way down the D 5 there is a metalled track which provides a convenient turning point. As you return through Lagnicourt note the large French Great War Memorial and the shells forming the supports for the chains. Follow the D 5 in the direction of Noreuil and Croisilles and, shortly after the sign post to Arras, turn left on to the D 36 to Vaulx-Vraucourt and Bapaume. The road climbs steadily and eventually, after about 3 kilometres, you will reach Vaulx Hill Cemetery on the right hand side of the road. This cemetery contains only seventeen graves from September 1918, in Plot I Rows A and B. The majority of the burials are as a result of concentrations after the Armistice. There are now 822 named graves (657 UK, 106 Australian, 58 New Zealand and 1 Canadian). There are also a number of unnamed graves and several special memorials. Among the Australians is Lieutenant-Colonel Bertram Watts DSO, commander of the 4th Field Artillery Brigade, killed near Lagnicourt on 10 April 1917. Other officers on his staff, killed at the same time, are buried nearby.

On the opposite of the road is the communal cemetery. Cross over the road and take the metalled track which runs alongside the cemetery. It goes down to a valley before rising to the Bois de Maricourt on the horizon. In the valley is the site of the Bois de Vaulx. The wood is no longer there but part of its shape is still shown on the IGN map as is a track, which led to one of its corners. This track is now called the Voie du Bois. In front of the wood were a series of trenches, the major one of which was Vaulx Trench. It was in this area that Prince Friedrich Karl of Prussia was forced to land, by Lieutenant Pickthorne of 32 Squadron, on 21 March 1917. The Australian troops, of the 26th Battalion, who fired on the Prince, were in Vaulx Trench.

Return to the main road and continue into Vaulx-Vraucourt. Follow

BOISE DE L'ERMITAGE   CEMETERY

Vraucourt Copse Cemetery and the Bois de l'Ermitage (Vraucourt Copse 1917) from the D 36E Vaulx-Vraucourt to Ecoust-St-Mein road.

the road round when it bears to the right: Ecoust-St-Mein, Bapaume, Ervillers. Turn sharp right again, ignore the signpost to Ecoust par CD 956, but turn right to remain on the D 36 to Ecoust-St-Mein. Shortly after leaving Vaulx-Vraucourt there is a Commonwealth War Graves sign, on the right hand of the road, to Vraucourt Copse Cemetery. The cemetery stands on a low ridge to the right of the road and is accessed along a track. The copse, after which it is named, is about 500 metres to the north and appears on the IGN map as Bois de l'Ermitage. The cemetery originally contained only 43 graves, originating from early September 1918, but in 1928 sixty more were added from Vaulx ADS Cemetery. The latter cemetery was on low and swampy ground, to the left of the road between Vraucourt Copse Cemetery and the village. Of the Australians buried here one is Second Lieutenant Richmond Gordon Howell-Price MC, 1st Battalion AIF, who died on 4 May 1917 as a result of wounds received, the previous day, at Bullecourt. He was one of three brothers killed in the war. Lieutenant-Colonel Owen Glendower Howell-Price DSO, MC, commanding the 3rd Battalion AIF, died of wounds on 4 November 1916 at Flers. He is buried at Heilly Station Cemetery, Méricourt-l'Abbé, France. The third brother, Major Philip Llewellyn Howell-Price DSO, MC, 1st Battalion AIF, was killed at Broodseinde on 4 October 1917. He is commemorated on the Menin Gate Memorial,Ypres, Belgium.

Continue on towards Ecoust-St-Mein. Shortly before reaching Longatte there is a large bunker on the right of the road, opposite a water tower. This bunker almost certainly dates from the Second World War. Just past the bunker, where the road joins the D 5, from Noreuil, turn left towards Croisilles. At the stop sign turn right on to the N 356 which shortly becomes the D 956. A straight stretch of road leads back to Bullecourt. As you near the village a line of trees, on either side of the road, marks the route of the Boisleux - Marquion railway. Further on, the road was crossed by the front trench of the Hindenburg Line, O.G.1 or Tower Trench. The ground between the trench line and the front part of the village constituted the 'Red Patch' **(See map 25)**. Just after reaching the village turn left, into the DC 10C, to Ecoust-St-Mein Gare. This is the Rue d'Arras. M. Jean Letaille, past Mayor of Bullecourt, lives in the first house on the right. It is here that he has the war museum. Continue down the road and turn left to pass the crucifix. The road now goes back to Ecoust-St-Mein, running parallel to the D 956. Carry on until you reach a stop sign, on the main road, where you turn right onto the D 5 to Croisilles and Arras. The communal cemetery is on the right with Ecoust-St-Mein British Cemetery in front of it. Beside the British cemetery is a track going off to the right. Take this track which rises steadily until it opens out and becomes a Chemin Privé. There is a large area for parking, near the line of the railway, from where you can view the ground, to the west of Bullecourt, over which the British 7th and 62nd Divisions operated.

Ecoust-St-Mein was captured by the 8th and 9th Battalions of the Devonshire Regiment, British 7th Division, in a blizzard on 2 April 1917. It was lost on 21 March 1918 but regained at the end of August 1918. The British Cemetery was begun in April 1917 and used by fighting units until March 1918. The remainder of the burials are as a result of concentration from neighbouring smaller burial grounds after the Armistice. On leaving the cemetery turn left back to Ecoust-St-Mein and return to Bullecourt either by taking the first or second turnings on the left.

Ecoust-St-Mein Communal Cemetery and the Ecoust British Cemetery.

Other cemeteries in the area

The following cemeteries, not covered in the tour, are well worth a visit. They can be reached by reference to the Commonwealth War Graves Commission map in conjunction with the IGN Blue Series map 2507 O (Croisilles).

H.A.C. Cemetery

It is located half a mile to the south of Ecoust-St-Mein on D956. It was begun by the 7th Division, after the capture of the village. The first burials were all members of the H.A.C. who fell in March and April 1917. After the German counter-attack at Lagnicourt, 15 April 1917, twelve Australian gunners were interred here in what is now Plot I Row A. In common with many other cemeteries it was extended, after the Armistice, and the register now records details of almost 2000 burials.

Ecoust Military Cemetery

Access is gained, from the village, along a grassy track passing close to someone's garden and the local sports field. It contains the graves of a number of the 2/6 North Staffs. Regiment who fell defending the nearby railway embankment in March 1918. Among them is the commanding officer Lieutenant-Colonel T.H.B. Thorne.

Noreuil Australian Cemetery

The cemetery lies to the south of Noreuil village. It was started at the beginning of April 1917 and used until the following December. The register records the details of 244 burials. Many of the bodies buried in early 1917 were destroyed by shell fire in later actions. In common with other cemeteries there are a number of special memorials to such lost graves. In this case the majority are to men of the Australian 50th Infantry Battalion.

Walk Number 1: The railway embankment and Igri Corner.

Walk time 1¹/₂ - 2 hours.
Maps: *IGN Blue Series 2507 O Croisilles.*   **Maps 32 and 9, 12, 18.**

For this walk a suitable place to park is on the right hand side of the D 956 between Ecoust-St-Mein and Bullecourt. The exact location is near the trees which mark the place where the Boisleux - Marquion railway crossed the road. The route of the old railway is barred to cars, by a large horizontal pole, but is accessible on foot. Take the track which, although flat at the start, soon rises to run along an embankment. It is easy to understand why dugouts were set into the

MAP 32: WALK 1 — THE RAILWAY, CENTRAL ROAD AND IGRI CORNER

Igri Corner, the site of Australian supply dump.

embankment, on the right, to seek shelter from the enemy observers and artillery. Bullecourt village is clearly visible on your left. As you move along the track reference to map 9 will enable you to identify the ground where the majority of the tanks involved on 11 April were put out of action. The embankment drops away and the ground becomes level as Riencourt church becomes visible to the left. Hendecourt is hidden behind the trees to the left of Riencourt. The line of the railway begins to swing to the right and that you are truly on an old railway is shown by the remains of sleepers under foot. The Digger memorial, and its accompanying flags, is also visible on the left. Remember that this memorial is in the ground between the two trenches of the Hindenburg Line.

Australian supply dump near Igri corner April 1917. IWM E(Aus)436

Eventually you will come to a semi-metalled track which joins from the right. This track does not appear on the trench maps of 1917 but in 1918 a trench, Tank Avenue, crossed the railway about here. Continue on past the track, following the path which now leaves the embankment but continues, along the edge of the field, to the right of the railway. From this lower level you get an even better idea of the security that was provided by the embankment. Soon the track begins to climb to reach another track which crosses the line of the one you are on. This was Central Road, which winds northwards towards Riencourt and southwards, back over the ridge, to Noreuil. The railway, at this point, is still overgrown and the track

145

seems to have stopped. However, it is possible to continue. If the ground is not too muddy, or overgrown, a walk along the edge of the field for about 200 metres will bring you to another track. Alternatively turn right on to Central Way and after about 200 metres turn left to return to the railway on the track just mentioned. This track runs parallel with Central Road up into Riencourt. From the point where the track crosses the railway Riencourt church is at 11 o'clock and the flags at the Digger memorial at about 9 o'clock. Between the flags and Bullecourt church the Sunken Road can be identified. It runs from Bullecourt across the open ground, parallel with the embankment, to cross Central Road and meet the track you are on. In 1917 it crossed the track and continued towards Quéant. It still continues eastward but from a point further up the track towards Riencourt. This sunken road is the one used by the Australians after it was found to be unoccupied by Captain Jacka **(See maps 12 and 18)**. In the ground between the two tracks Jacka, again, went out into No Man's Land on 9 April to examine, and report on, the state of the defences opposite the Australian 4th Brigade. It was across the same ground that Captain Gilchrist led the men of the Australian 5th Brigade on 3 May 1917. To the left of the track the ground rises and here, at the wire between O.G.1 and O.G.2, Major Percy Black, 16th Battalion AIF, was killed.

Return to the point where the track is joined by Central Road. Continue on the track until you come to a cross road of tracks and turn left. After about 200 metres the track starts to drop down into the Noreuil valley and becomes sunken on both sides. After a short descent you come to signpost 'Sentier du Bois Gilles 7 km'. A few more steps and the track bears to the right but a lesser one continues across the valley. It was here that Captain Sheppard faced the German machine gun, across the valley, on 15 April 1917. Retrace your steps back to the track cross roads. If you continue on the same track you will be heading for point 94 and the spot where you parked. However, to visit Igri Corner turn left on to the metalled road. As you walk towards Noreuil note the field on the left, edged with barbed wire supported by screw pickets, with posts made from old railway line. On reaching Igri Corner, where the Australians established their major supply dump, turn right and walk up the hill. On reaching the crest Bullecourt church is directly ahead and the road leading to it becomes sunken providing good cover for troops carry supplies forward from the Igri Corner dump. As the road bears to the right a clump of willow trees marks the site of a hole on the left hand side of the road. It was here, or close by, that a large explosion took place on the evening of 6 May 1917.

To assist the British 7th Division, Z Company, Special Brigade Royal Engineers, was ordered to attack two strong points on the southern edge of Bullecourt village at 3.45 a.m. on the morning of 7 May 1917 using gas projectors. Developed by William Livens, projectors, first used at Arras on 4 April 1917, consisted of an 8 inch solid steel tube, 2 feet 9 inches or 4 feet long, 1/4 inch thickness and closed at one end. The tube was buried up to the nozzle in a trench cut at an angle of 45°. The force of the recoil was absorbed by a metal base-plate. Projectors were fired in batteries of 25 closely packed together. The projectile was a gas drum about twenty inches long which contained about 30 lbs. of liquid phosgene. The drums, complete with a special bursting charge, fitted loosely into the projector to allow electric leads to pass down the sides into boxes containing the propellant charges. The projectors were linked to each other and to a central firing point.

In preparation Z Company assembled 250 projectors, high explosive bombs, propellants and detonators to be transported, by 20 four-horse General Service wagons, to a forward position, a short distance behind the firing position. The firing position was just back from point 94 to the left of the track and the off-loading point to the right of the track. All went well with the first ten wagons, which contained projectors, save one which had to abandoned, close to the off-loading point, when one of the horses was wounded. Carrying-parties started to transport the bombs forward as two more wagons arrived bearing the propellant charges followed by four more carrying bombs. It was at this point that disaster struck. A German shell either struck a wagon containing the propellant charges or exploded close by setting off the charges. The enemy, alerted by the explosions, immediately deluged the area with artillery fire. The officer in charge, Second Lieutenant S. Oakes was killed along with 7 other ranks from Z Company. All are buried together in Beaulencourt British Cemetery, Ligny-Thilloy. In all over 80 casualties were recorded. It

Eleven casualties from the Special Brigade accident, Beaulencourt British Cemetery, Ligny - Thilloy.

Site of the Special Brigade accident in May 1917.

was the worst accident experienced by the Special Brigade during the war.

The war diary places the site of the accident in the area to the right of the track. But, given the errors that often occur and the fact that the wagons were coming along the track from Noreuil, it is possible that the large hole near the willows is, in fact, a crater resulting from the explosions and subsequent artillery pounding.

Continue on up to point 94 where you will join the track, noted earlier, coming from the track cross roads. Follow the metalled road round towards the D 956 and your parking spot. As you do this Bullecourt church is again visible and the line of the railway embankment is defined by the line of trees running along it. Breaks in the trees, where Central Road and the adjacent track cross the line, can also be seen.

Walk Number 2: Diagonal Road, Central Road and the Sunken Road.

Walk time 1¹⁄₂ - 2 hours.
Maps: *IGN Blue Series 2507 O Croisilles.* **Maps 33 and 19**

Drive to Bullecourt and park beside the church, the site of the village pond in 1917. On the opposite side of the road is the Mairie and the village war memorial. Inside the Mairie the picture by James Scott, representing the death of Major Percy Black, presented to the village

Bullecourt church before the war.

Bullecourt church April 1917. German official photograph.
IWMQ45458

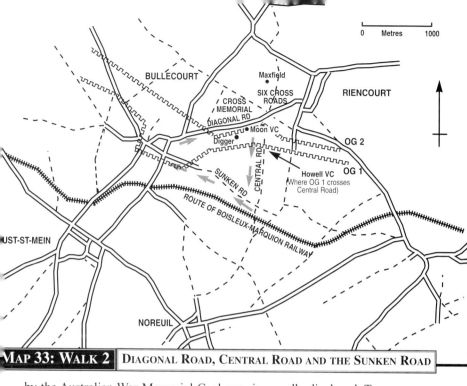

Map labels: BULLECOURT, Maxfield, SIX CROSS ROADS, RIENCOURT, CROSS MEMORIAL, DIAGONAL RD, Moon VC, Digger, OG 2, CENTRAL RD, SUNKEN RD, Howell VC (Where OG 1 crosses Central Road), OG 1, ROUTE OF BOISLEUX-MARQUION RAILWAY, UST-ST-MEIN, NOREUIL

0   Metres   1000

MAP 33: WALK 2 | DIAGONAL ROAD, CENTRAL ROAD AND THE SUNKEN ROAD

by the Australian War Memorial Canberra, is proudly displayed. Turn left to pass the Slouch Hat Memorial which commemorates the Australian and British soldiers who fell in the area in April and May 1917. The memorial, erected by the Souvenir Française in 1981,

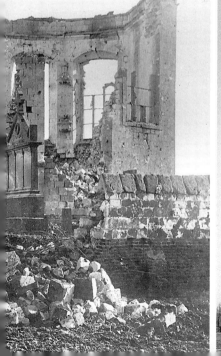

Bullecourt church in 1992

The Slouch Hat Memorial at Bullecourt

displays the badge of the AIF together with the divisional signs of the three British divisions involved. Continue along the road until you come to a turning, going off to the right, the Rue des Australiens. There is also a sign directing you to the Bullecourt Australian Memorial. As you walk towards the memorial, which with its two accompanying flags is to the right of the road, Riencourt church is directly in front. The memorial stands in what was ground between the two trenches of the Hindenburg Line. It was erected by the Australian Department of Veteran Affairs and dedicated on 25 April 1992. The plaque carries the following dedication in English and French.

Sacred to the memory of the 10,00 members of the
Australian Imperial Force who were killed and wounded
in the two battles of Bullecourt, April to May 1917, and
to the Australian dead and the comrades in arms who
lie here forever in the soil of France.
"Lest We Forget"

At the entrance to the memorial there is another plaque, one of the many created by Ross Bastiaan. It was unveiled by Senator, the Hon. John Faulkner, Minister for Veteran Affairs, 2nd September 1993. It is an orientation table which shows the line of the furthest German advance, and the direction of the German offensive, in 1918. It also a

Bullecourt Rue de Quéant, which becomes the Sunken Road.

Rue de Quéant Bullecourt before the war.

describes the Allied offensive around Arras and Vimy in April 1917. Ross Bastiaan is a periodontist in private practice in Melbourne Australia. In 1987, whilst visiting Gallipoli, Dr Bastiaan was struck by the lack of information presented to English-speaking visitors to the battlefields. Three years later the first of his plaques was erected at Anzac Cove, one of ten now on the Gallipoli peninsula. Since then the project has burgeoned to cover Australian actions in many parts of the world.

Return to the road and turn right to continue in the same direction. The road marks the line of O.G.2, which joined it at the Cross Memorial and ran along the road before turning to pass behind the village. It was at the junction, with Diagonal Road, that the Australians were held up in both battles due to the problem presented by the trench and road being at different levels. As you walk towards the Cross Memorial the line of trees marking the line railway can be seen drifting back towards the horizon. Just before you reach the memorial the sunken part of Central Road can be seen running into Diagonal Road from the direction of the railway embankment. The Cross Memorial, like the Slouch Hat Memorial, was erected by the Arras branch of the Souvenir Française, lead by M. André Coilliot. Since the erection of the memorial numerous visitors have added their own tributes.

In memory of
all my mates killed in action
lest we forget
R.M. Gunn 4th AIF

It was also close to the junction that Lieutenant Rupert Moon won the Victoria Cross. Continue on the road which now drops down and swings round to bring you to the Six Cross Roads. As you approach the junction the scene of Captain Maxfield's exploit is in the field to your left at about 11 o'clock. The

The Cross Memorial at Bullecourt.

trench tramway which ran beside O.G.1 cut across O.G.2 in the field to your right before crossing the road just in front of the Six Cross Roads **(See map 19)**. There are now only five roads at the junction but the road not reinstated is shown on map 33. Turn right on to the track which is Central Road. The track climbs gently and shortly you can see the line of trees on the railway embankment. O.G.2 crossed the track

151

near the clump of shrubs on the right hand side. Once past the shrubs you are walking in the ground between O.G.1 and O.G.2. The land on the right remains flat and Bullecourt is clearly visible but on the left it rises quite steeply and afforded protection to the Australians seeking shelter from fire coming from Riencourt and Quéant. Shortly there is a kink in the track where it bears left and almost immediately to the right. It was about here that O.G.1 crossed and Corporal Howell won the Victoria Cross. From here Pioneer Trench ran back to the railway embankment beside Central Road. Further down Central Road the bank on the left begins to fall away until, at the junction with the a metalled road on the right, it is level. When you reach the metalled road turn right. This is the Sunken Road occupied by the Australian troops following Captain Jacka's reconnaissance into No Man's Land **(See maps 12 and 18)**. In the distance the road can be seen to become deeply sunken indicating how it achieved its name. Many troops took cover in the sunken area before moving out, into the land on the right, before the attacks. Continue on the track until it enters Bullecourt village, where it is known as the Rue de Quéant. At the junction with the main road turn right and make your way back to the church.

Walk Number 3: Copse Trench and the Crucifix.

Walk time 1½ hours.
Maps: *IGN Blue Series 2507 O Croisilles.* **Maps 34 and 25, 21, 8**

This is a short walk which covers the ground to the north-west of Bullecourt. Towards the end of the walk a north-south view of the British 62nd Division area of operations, will be obtained. This should be compared with the opposite view from Ecoust-St-Mein, which is part of the general tour.

The most convenient parking place is again beside the church in Bullecourt. Turn right and follow the route towards the Digger memorial given in walk No. 2. This was the Brown Line for the attack on 7 May **(See map 25).** After reaching the Rue des Australiens and starting to climb towards the Digger memorial take the track which goes off on the left hand side of the road. Keep to the right of the track avoiding the section which drops down on to the left. You are at point U.22.d.0.3 **(See map 21)** where O.G.2, left the line of the road to run behind

The Digger Memorial
at Bullecourt

Bullecourt village. The track climbs steadily to a point where there is a steep drop on the left hand side. Continue along the track until you come to a T-junction with another track. Between the junction and the point at which the ground became level the trench tramway crossed the track. This tramway ran from O.G.1 to O.G.2, near Central Road and, on to the Six Cross Roads before turning to run parallel with the Hindenburg Line. It finally turned to the left to enter Bullecourt on the western side. In the ground near the junction, to the right of the track from the Six Cross Roads,

The line of the track running back to the Six Cross Roads from D956 Hendecourt - Bullecourt road.

was a complex of deep German dugouts, according to reports from the Australian 24th Battalion However, no sign of these dugouts is now visible. Turn left and walk along the track to the point where it crosses the D 956 from Bullecourt to Hendecourt. Cross over the road and continue along the track, which is no longer metalled. Once over the road the track becomes sunken on both sides and climbs steadily. At the summit the spire of the church at Fontaine-lès-Croisilles is directly ahead and, the water tower at Hendecourt at about 3 o'clock. In the

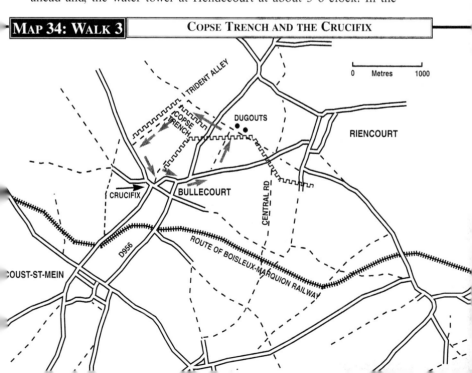

ground to your left the trenches of the Artillerie Schutzstellung ran back to Fontaine-lès-Croisilles **(See map 8)**. A section of the line is shown on map 34 as Copse Trench. Continue on the track until it is joined by a metalled track on the left hand side. Take this track and head towards Ecoust-St-Mein. Trident Alley, a communication trench which joined the Hindenburg Line with the Artillerie Schutzstellung and Hendecourt, followed the line of this track. The track was crossed by O.G.1 and O.G.2 just before joining the road from Fontaine-lès-Croisilles to Bullecourt. From this point Ecoust church is at 11 o'clock. The ground drops away and rises up to the line of the Boisleux - Marquion railway shown by the line of trees. The British 62nd Division starting lines were approximately half way between the railway and the road **(See map 21)**. Contrast this view, from the north, with the one from the south in the general battlefield tour. Turn left on to this road and head back towards Bullecourt. The road is joined by a track on the right and shortly the Crucifix is on your right. Note the large horse chestnut tree which grows on the site. In 1916 the children

The Crucifix before the war.

of Bullecourt used to climb the original to watch the battle of the Somme. Continue straight across the junction to join the main road through the village. Turn left, on to the N 356 towards Hendecourt and Douai, and a short walk will bring you back to the church.

The Crucifix at Bullecourt.

APPENDIX ONE

Order of Battle: Fifth Army April 1917

G.O.C. General Sir Hubert Gough.

Chief of Staff: Major-General Neill Malcolm.

V Corps: Lieutenant-General Sir Edward Fanshawe.

7th DIVISION: Major-General T.H. Shoubridge.

20th Brigade	*22nd Brigade*	*91st Brigade*
2/Borders.	2/Royal Warwicks.	2/Queen's.
2/Gordon H.	1/R.W.F.	1/S.Staffs.
8/Devons.	20/Manchesters.	21/Manchesters.
9/Devons.	2/H.A.C.	22/Manchesters.

58th (2/1 LONDON) DIVISION: Major-General H.D. Fanshawe.

173rd Brigade	*174th Brigade*	*175th Brigade*
2/1 London.	2/5 London.	2/9 London.
2/2 London.	2/6 London.	2/10 London.
2/3 London.	2/7 London.	2/11 London.
2/4 London.	2/8 London.	2/12 London.

62nd (WEST RIDING) DIVISON: Major-General W.P. Braithwaite.

185th Brigade	*186th Brigade*	*187th Brigade*
2/5 West Yorks.	2/4 Duke of Wellington's.	2/4 KOYLI.
2/6 West Yorks.	2/5 Duke of Wellington's.	2/5 KOYLI.
2/7 West Yorks.	2/6 Duke of Wellington's.	2/4 Y & L.
2/8 West Yorks.	2/7 Duke of Wellington's.	2/5 Y & L.

1 Anzac Corps: Lieutenant-General Sir William Birdwood.

1st AUSTRALIAN DIVISION: Major-General H.B. Walker.

1st (N.S.W.) Brigade	*2nd (Victoria) Brigade*	*3rd Brigade*
1st Battalion.	5th Battalion.	9th (Q'land) Bn.
2nd Battalion.	6th Battalion.	10th (S. Austr.) Bn.
3rd Battalion.	7th Battalion.	11th (W Austr.) Bn.
4th Battalion.	8th Battalion.	12th (S & W Austr., Tas.) Bn.

2nd AUSTRALIAN DIVISION: Major-General N. Smyth.VC

5th (N.S.W.) Brigade	*6th (Victoria) Brigade*	*7th Brigade*
17th Battalion.	21st Battalion.	25th (Q'land) Bn.
18th Battalion.	22nd Battalion.	26th (Q'land, Tas.)Bn.
19th Battalion.	23rd Battalion.	27th (S.Austr.) Bn.
20th Battalion.	24th Battalion.	28th (W.Austr.)Bn.

4th AUSTRALIAN DIVISION: Major-General W. Holmes.

4th Brigade	*12th Brigade*	*13th Brigade*
13th (N.S.W.) Bn.	45th (N.S.W.) Bn.	49th (Q'land) Bn.
14th (Vic.) Bn.	46th (Vic.) Bn.	50th (S.Austr.) Bn.

15th (Q'land, Tas.) Bn.	47th (Q'land, Tas.) Bn.	51st (W.Austr.) Bn.
16th (S.& W. Austr.) Bn.	48th (S.& W. Austr.) Bn.	52nd (S.& W. Austr., Tas.) Bn.

5th AUSTRALIAN DIVISION: Major-General J.J.T. Hobbs.

8th Brigade	*14th (N.S.W.) Brigade*	*15th (Victoria) Bde.*
29th (Vic.) Bn.	53rd Battalion.	57th Battalion.
30th (N.S.W.) Bn.	54th Battalion.	58th Battalion.
31st (Q'land, Vic.) Bn.	55th Battalion.	59th Battalion.
32nd (S. & W. Austr.) Bn.	56th Battalion.	60th Battalion.

APPENDIX TWO

The 62nd (West Riding) Division.

This was a 2nd-line (or reserve) Territorial Force division and had no existence before the outbreak of war. The formation of such 2nd line units was authorised on 31 August 1914. The twelve infantry battalions were raised in September and October 1914 and eventually brigaded as the 185th, 186th and 187th Brigades (See Appendix 1). By November 1914, battalions were able to furnish drafts to their first-line formations, but it was not until December 1916 that orders were received that the division was to be ready to embark for France on 5 January 1917. Between February and March 1917 the division was engaged in operations on the Ancre, as part of the Fifth Army and following the German retreat took up its position in front of Bullecourt.

The 58th (2nd/1st London) Division.

Like the 62nd Division, the 58th was a second line (or reserve) Territorial Force division and had no existence before the outbreak of war. The division came into being following the re-deployment, between September 1914 and January 1915, of ten battalions of the 1st London Division. The remaining two battalions along with the G.O.C., G.S.O.1., B.G., R.A., C.R.E., heavy battery, and the signal company, amalgamated with the 2nd-line units of the London Division to form the new division. The field artillery of the 1st London Division joined them in August 1915.

When, in 1915, the division was brigaded as 173rd, 174th and 175th, the four City of London Battalions, Royal Fusiliers, had already been sent, as replacements, to Malta. The 173rd brigade, was therefore allocated the corresponding third line units which were redesignated second line units in June 1916.

In the Spring of 1916 the division was fully equipped and embarked upon a final training programme. It eventually embarked for France on 20 January 1917 but delays occurred during the crossings, and so it was not until 8 February that the division concentrated around Lucheux, in XVIII Corps area. On 19 March it transferred to VII Corps before becoming involved in the fighting for Bullecourt with the 1st Anzac corps.

In Appendix 1, the battalions in the 174th and 175th Brigades are, simply referred to as 2/5 - 2/8 and 2/9 - 2/12 London Battalions respectively. Their full titles are:

2/5 (City of London). Battalion. (London Rifle Brigade).
2/6 (City of London). Battalion. (Rifles).
2/7 (City of London). Battalion.
2/8 (City of London). Battalion. (Post Office Rifles).

2/9 (County of London). Battalion. (Queen Victoria's Rifles).
2/10 (County of London). Battalion. (Hackney).
2/11 (County of London). Battalion. (Finsbury Rifles).
2/12 (County of London). Battalion. (The Rangers).

APPENDIX THREE

Villers-Bretonneux Military Cemetery and the Australian National Memorial are situated at Fouilloy, ten miles east of Amiens and a little north of the main road to St. Quentin. The cemetery, in front of the memorial, contains over 2000 graves and was created by concentration from a wide area after the end of the war. The memorial is dedicated to the Australian soldiers who fought in France and Belgium, to their dead, and especially to those dead whose graves are unknown. The bodies of many of the Australians who were killed at Bullecourt were either not recovered or destroyed in later fighting. The memorial, designed by Sir Edwin Lutyens, is in the form of a bell-tower 100 feet high with flanking walls. The memorial panels, beneath the tower, carry in excess of 10,000 names.

Australian soldiers, mentioned in the text, whose names are recorded on the Villers-Bretonneux Memorial:

Major P.C.H. Black. DSO, DCM, Croix de Guerre(Fr).16th Battalion.
Lieutenant C.H. Dakin. 5th Company Machine Gun Corps.
Lieutenant R.D. Desmond. 5th Company Machine Gun Corps.
Lieutenant P.G.D Fethers. 24th Battalion.
Captain W.R. Gilchrist. MC. 6th Field Company Engineers.
Lieutenant J. Harris. 24th Battalion.
Lieutenant J.E. Jennings. 21st Battalion.
Private A.W. King. 2675 57th Battalion.
Second Lieutenant R.J. Lanyon. 28th Battalion.
Captain G.L. Maxfield. MC. 24th Battalion.
Lieutenant D.J. Rentoul MC. 2nd Division Signal Company Engineers.
Second Lieutenant H.L. Rhynehart. 24th Battalion.
Sergeant L.G. Scott. 366 12th Battalion.
Lieutenant R. Sherwin. MC. 12th Battalion.
Lieutenant S.J. Topp 58th Battalion.

FURTHER READING

1. *The Official History of Australia in the War 1914 - 1918.* Volume IV.
The A.I.F. in France 1917. C.E.W. Bean. 1933.
Also available in soft back from University of Queensland Press. 1980.
A very detailed account of both the battles of Bullecourt and the German counter-attack at Lagnicourt. There are numerous maps and footnotes but the style is such that it does not make easy reading.
2. *Official History of the War. Military Operations in France and Belgium, 1917.*
Volume I. Captain Cyril Falls. Macmillan 1940.
3. *The Blood Tub. General Gough and the Battle of Bullecourt 1917.*
Jonathan Walker. Spellmount 1998.
An excellent account of the fighting at Bullecourt but with, as the title indicates, the accent on the behaviour of General Gough.
4. *Prelude to Victory.* E.L. Spears. Jonathan Cape 1939.
5. *Cheerful Sacrifice. The Battle of Arras 1917.* Jonathan Nicholls. Leo Cooper 1990.
A very full account of the Arras fighting with several references to Bullecourt.
6. *Before Endeavours Fade.* A Guide to the Battlefields of the First World War.
Rose Coombs.
Originally published in the early 1980s but recently completely updated. Covers all the important sites in France and Belgium.
7. *A Guidebook to Australian Battlefields of the Western Front 1914 - 1918.*
John Laffin.
An Australian view of the battlefields.
8. Other volumes in the Battleground Europe Series, particularly: *The Hindenburg Line* by Peter Oldham and *Vimy Ridge* by Nigel Cave.

Selective Index

Lossberg, Colonel Fritz von, 20
Louverval, 70, 131
Mackay, Lieutenant - Colonel I., 102
Malcolm, Major - General N., 32, 42
Maxfield, Captain G.L., 83, 84, 86, 151
Memorials:
    Cross, 58, 135, 151
    Digger, 135, 146, 152
    Slouch Hat, 149, 150
    Villers-Bretonneux, 111, 157
Military Units: Australian:
Divisions:
    1st, 69, 70 - 72, 97
    2nd, 69, 70 - 72, 79, 80, 81
    4th, 33, 39, 45, 69
    5th, 111
Brigades:
    1st, 70, 72 - 74, 97, 100, 102, 111
    2nd, 70, 72, 73, 111
    3rd, 70, 71, 103
    4th, 39, 41, 49, 56, 57, 61
    5th, 69, 74, 81, 83, 86, 94, 95, 97,
        117, 119
    6th, 69, 81, 83, 94, 95, 97, 118
    7th, 81, 86, 95
    8th, 114
    12th, 39, 49, 56 - 59, 61
Battalions:
    1st, 40, 97, 100 - 102, 110, 132
    2nd, 70, 100, 102, 110
    3rd, 70, 71, 97, 100 - 102, 110
    4th, 70, 71, 102, 110
    9th, 70, 74, 110
    10th, 70
    11th, 70, 102, 103, 130
    12th, 70, 72, 73, 102, 103, 127, 129
    13th, 39, 41, 56, 57, 61
    14th, 39, 40, 41, 48, 56, 57
    15th, 39, 41, 56, 57
    16th, 39, 40, 41, 48, 56, 57
    17th, 70 - 73, 81
    18th, 70, 81, 82
    19th, 70, 74, 81
    20th, 70, 74, 81
    21st, 81, 84
    22nd, 81,84
    23rd, 81, 83, 84
    24th, 81, 83, 84, 153
    25th, 95
    26th, 81, 96
    28th, 86, 95, 97, 102
    54th, 114

57th, 111
    58th, 111, 113, 133
Military Units: British:
Armies:
    First, 31,78
    Third, 25, 27, 32, 78, 88, 90
    Fifth, 25, 27, 32, 69, 78, 114
Divisions:
    7th, 9, 45, 94, 98, 104, 110, 111
    21st, 45
    58th, 9, 109, 112
    62nd, 9,33, 39, 45 - 48, 62, 65, 69, 79,
        80, 86, 88, 90, 92, 94, 95, 107,
        116, 152, 154
Brigades:
    20th, 104, 107
    22nd, 45, 98, 104, 108
    91st, 107, 1089
    173rd, 109, 112 - 114
    174th, 114
    175th, 114
    185th, 45, 62, 91, 94, 116
    186th, 91 - 94, 116
    187th, 91 - 94, 116
Battalions:
    2/Borders, 106
    8/Devons, 105 - 107
    9/Devons, 104 - 107
    2/4 Duke of Wellington's, 91
    2/5 Duke of Wellington's, 91 - 93
    2/6 Duke of Wellington's, 91,92
    2/7 Duke of Wellington's, 91
    2/Gordons, 104, 110
    2/H.A.C., 98, 106, 109
    2/4 KOYLI, 91
    2/5 KOYLI, 91,93
    2/3 London, 114
    2/4 London, 114
    2/5 London, 114
    2/8 London, 114
    20/Manchesters, 98,109
    21/Manchesters, 107
    22/Manchesters, 107, 108
    2/Queen's, 107 - 109, 112
    2/Royal Warwicks, 98, 100 108
    1/Royal Welch Fusiliers, 98, 100, 109
    1/South Staffs., 107,108
    2/5 West Yorks., 45, 46, 91, 93
    2/6 West Yorks., 62, 91, 93, 94
    2/7 West Yorks., 45, 46, 91, 93
    2/8 West Yorks., 45, 46, 62, 91, 93
    2/4 Yorks & Lancs., 92